INSIGHT 👁 EDITIONS
PO Box 3088
San Rafael, CA 94912
www.insighteditions.com

Library of Congress Cataloging-in-Publication Data available.
ISBN: 978-1-60887-104-9

Design by Jon Glick
Text by Brandon T. Snider
Special thanks to Shane Thompson, Izzy Hyams,
Jill Benscoter, Josh Anderson, Amy Wideman,
and Christopher Cerasi

Batman created by Bob Kane

Manufactured in China by Insight Editions

THE DARK KNIGHT MANUAL

TOOLS, WEAPONS, VEHICLES & DOCUMENTS FROM THE BATCAVE

INSIGHT EDITIONS

San Rafael, California

CONTENTS

City of Gotham Police Department

WAYNE MURDER REPORT

Sgt. James Gordon
Responding Officer's Report
Case #111939

At approximately 10:35 PM on the night of November 8, Thomas and Martha Wayne, accompanied by their son, Bruce, left the Gotham Opera House by a service exit on the south side of the building. Why the Waynes chose to leave by this exit is unclear, but it's possible they were hoping to avoid the cameras of various paparazzi that had gathered at the theater in light of the family being in attendance. Regardless of their reason, the family exited into the area commonly known as "Crime Alley" and were shortly thereafter approached by the suspect.

At approximately 10:40 PM, the suspect (recorded by surveillance cameras as having shaggy blond hair and wearing an oversized green coat) approached the family, produced a gun (identified by ballistics as a Nagant M1895 revolver), and asked the family to give up their valuables. The boy reports that the suspect seemed hurried and agitated and smelled of alcohol. By his account, the suspect advanced on Martha Wayne and when he did so, Thomas Wayne stepped in the way. This is when the first shot occurred, striking Mr. Wayne in the chest. From the placement of the bodies and the boy's recollection of events, we can ascertain that Martha went to cover her husband as he fell to the ground. From the pearls littering the scene, we believe that there was a struggle for Mrs. Wayne's necklace, at which point the suspect shot her through the chest, killing her instantly. The suspect then fled the scene, escaping with only the wallet of Mr. Wayne.

Ballistics found two spent cartridges at the scene that point to the use of the revolver mentioned previously in the report. Paramedics responding to the crime scene found both Thomas and Martha Wayne dead upon their arrival and the young boy in a state of shock. They estimate the time of death for Mrs. Wayne was 10:49 PM and the time of death for Mr. Wayne 10:47 PM.

The GPD currently has one suspect in custody in the murder of Thomas and Martha Wayne. The boy is being remanded to the care of the family's longtime butler, Alfred Pennyworth.

City of Gotham Police Department

REPORT OF EXAMINATION

To: Gotham PD
Major Crimes Unit
Officer Ronald Probson

Date: June 29, 1984
Case ID No: 89B-DX-86010

Lab No. 101217002 GC NN

Title: UNBXT(S);
    THOMAS WAYNE- VICTIM A (DECEASED); MARTHA WAYNE- VICTIM B (DECEASED);
    ASSAULT OF AN UNARMED CIVILIAN, TWO COUNTS

The following items were examined in the Firearm/Ballistics Unit:

Q1   Nagant M1895 revolver (double-action)
Q2.1   Cartridge (1) from Q1 (1B2, E4418572, Item 1)
Q2.2   Cartridge (2) from Q1 (1B5, E4418573, Item 2)
Q3   Bullet from victim A (1B7, E4418575)
Q4   Bullet from victim B (1B7, E4418576)

Specimens Q2.1 and Q2.2 are 7.62x38mmR cartridges loaded with copper-washed
steel jacketed bullets that were fired from a barrel rifled with four grooves,
right twist, and bear the headstamp of the Federal State Enterprise Vymple,
Russia. The Q2.1 through Q2.2 cartridges have the physical characteristics of
functional ammunition. Examination of the Nagant M1895 found no indication that
the weapon had been altered to fire additional cartridges with a single pull of
the trigger. A search of the FBI laboratory's Reference Ammunition File found
cartridges similar to specimens Q2.1 through Q2.2 marketed under the name of
Golden Dragon Ammunition.

Supporting documentation for the examinations conducted for this report is
retained in the GPD Laboratory files. The submitted items will be returned by
the Laboratory's Evidence Control Unit (GPD-0401). For questions about the
content of this report, please contact Officer Travis Geoffry. For questions
concerning the disposition of the items, please contact Request Coordinator
Percy Luck.

For Official Use Only

CASE CLOSED

GOTHAM POST

MIDTOWN EDITION

Overcast; chance of precipitation this afternoon / Weather: Page 55 • • • • 75¢

CHAOS SWEEPS GOTHAM

TRAINING

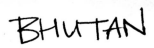

BHUTAN

...THE DRIVE TO DO GREAT OR
TERRIBLE THINGS... YOU MUST
JOURNEY INWARDS...

I traveled the Far East for a long time before I met the man known as Rā's al Ghūl and the men loyal to him, the League of Shadows. When Rā's found me I was spending aimless time in prison, doing little more than defending myself from those who felt superior or were physically intimidating. I was aggressive but lacked discipline. Rā's saw in me a malleable form, someone he could mold and use for his own purposes. He saw potential.

The greatest lesson I absorbed in Bhutan was how to unlock the power of my mind as well as my body. I had long been filled with fear and anger and thought that allowing myself to access these emotions would render me vulnerable, weak. But Rā's showed me a way to embrace my fears, to reject all hesitation and to focus, unwavering, on the task at hand.

Deception was perhaps Rā's al Ghūl's favorite trick. He led me to believe he had my best interests at heart when I was simply a pawn in his game to destroy Gotham City. But despite his ultimate betrayal, I learned from him a number of important lessons and gained much of value from our time together. Although it was certainly not his intention, his training helped me on the road to becoming Batman.

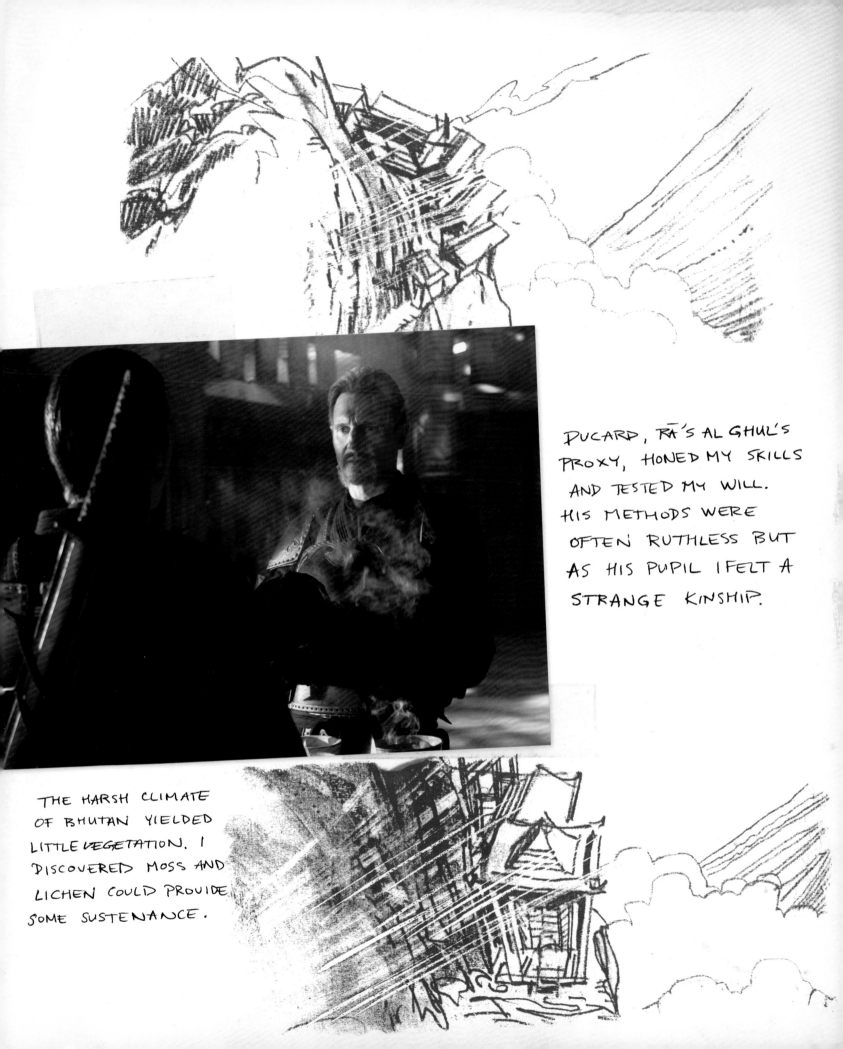

DUCARD, RĀ'S AL GHUL'S PROXY, HONED MY SKILLS AND TESTED MY WILL. HIS METHODS WERE OFTEN RUTHLESS BUT AS HIS PUPIL I FELT A STRANGE KINSHIP.

THE HARSH CLIMATE OF BHUTAN YIELDED LITTLE VEGETATION. I DISCOVERED MOSS AND LICHEN COULD PROVIDE SOME SUSTENANCE.

FIGHTING TECHNIQUES

Self-defense requires great patience and discipline.

You must learn to both temper your anger and to channel it; master defensive postures as well as offensive maneuvers. Gauging one's true competence is difficult unless one is put in a position where defense is required. Martial arts allow the student to open his mind and body in tandem so that his entire being works as a single unit, preparing him for the unexpected. The opportunity for physical and spiritual growth through martial arts is immense and should be treated with respect and commitment.

NINJA/NINJITSU—*THE WRAITH*

A ninja can move in circles undetected or boldly infiltrate a group and destroy it from within. In feudal Japan, the ninja were masters of guerilla warfare who could become anything and be anyone. Their methods were dark and sometimes arcane. Ninja were known to plot bold, elaborate strategies and execute them stealthily over a period of time. Their training sculpts them into something mysterious and wraithlike.

The ninja is thought invisible. But invisibility, as I was taught, is largely a matter of patience.

FROM THE DESK OF
BRUCE WAYNE

YOUR ANGER GIVES YOU GREAT POWER, BUT IF YOU LET IT, IT WILL DESTROY YOU.

JIUJITSU—*FLEXIBLE TECHNIQUE*

This Japanese martial art focuses on manipulating an opponent's force against him. Most commonly practiced in close combat, the discipline is invaluable when caught weaponless in the face of an armed opponent. An enemy wielding a weapon often expects a counterattack, retaliation, but jiujitsu is subtle and unexpected. It pinpoints an enemy's weaknesses and exploits them. A fist isn't just blocked; it can be trapped and deflected back. A brawl can be defused quickly using these methods.

SPARRING WITH LEAGUE MEMBERS FORCED ME TO CALL ON EVERY AVAILABLE DISCIPLINE.

BASIC DRESS IS A SIMPLE GI
WORN UNDER A TRADITIONAL
LEATHER VEST WITH CHEST
AND SHOULDER PADDING. BUT
MANY LEAGUE MEMBERS
DEVIATE FROM THIS IN
FAVOR OF THEIR OWN
CLOTHING.

THE LEAGUE FAVORED
LEATHER MASKS AND
BLACK FABRIC HOODS
THAT WERE LOOSE
AROUND THE NECK AREA
AND FORMFITTING
AROUND THE HEAD,
LEAVING THE MEREST
SLIT FOR EYES.

THE LEAGUE OF SHADOWS

SOME LEAGUE MEMBERS WEAR ORNATE
GAUNTLETS, PERHAPS CENTURIES OLD,
WITH JAGGED, TALONLIKE SPIKES. THE
GAUNTLET SHIELDS AND DEFLECTS ATTACKS
FROM KATANA AND SIMILAR BLADES.

BASE OF OPERATIONS

Billionaire Absconds With Entire Moscow Ballet

...Russian Ballet Artistic ...rector and Choreographer Grace Benz

Photograph by Ben Nowicki for the G...

the
...am
...am

...t the
...rked
...pher
...let's
...pany
...am
...ent a

...rts in
...ding
...ssian
But
...from
...who's
...more
...siness

City
...years
...uction
...th it.
...b the
...e the
...ter is

Photograph by James Mcallister for the Gotham Times.

Bruce Wayne's 100 foot yacht, has been nicknamed 'The Love Boat'.

...lmination or a transformation. But in... absolute control over their company and

I returned to Gotham City from Bhutan with one goal: to build a crime-fighting operation. I began mapping out what I needed in terms of equipment—weaponry, armor, transportation—and who I could trust to help me obtain it.

Former Wayne Enterprises CEO William Earle had billed Applied Sciences, the company's Research and Development wing, a "dead end" filled with failed experiments and novel military items. A number of the company's developments had simply been shelved and long forgotten—protective armor, medicinal injectors, and even all-terrain vehicles were seen as too experimental and too expensive to produce. Wayne Enterprises' history was built on groundbreaking technologies that had moved the company into position as a major player in a variety of global markets, as well as a coveted military contractor. Access to these would prove invaluable.

The head of Applied Sciences, Lucius Fox, worked for my father for years and even helped him build the Gotham Monorail. He was eventually promoted to CEO when Earle stepped down. Together, Lucius and I would build our headquarters.

WAYNE ENTERPRISES
APPLIED SCIENCES DIVISION

BRUCE WAYNE
CDØNBCKCVR

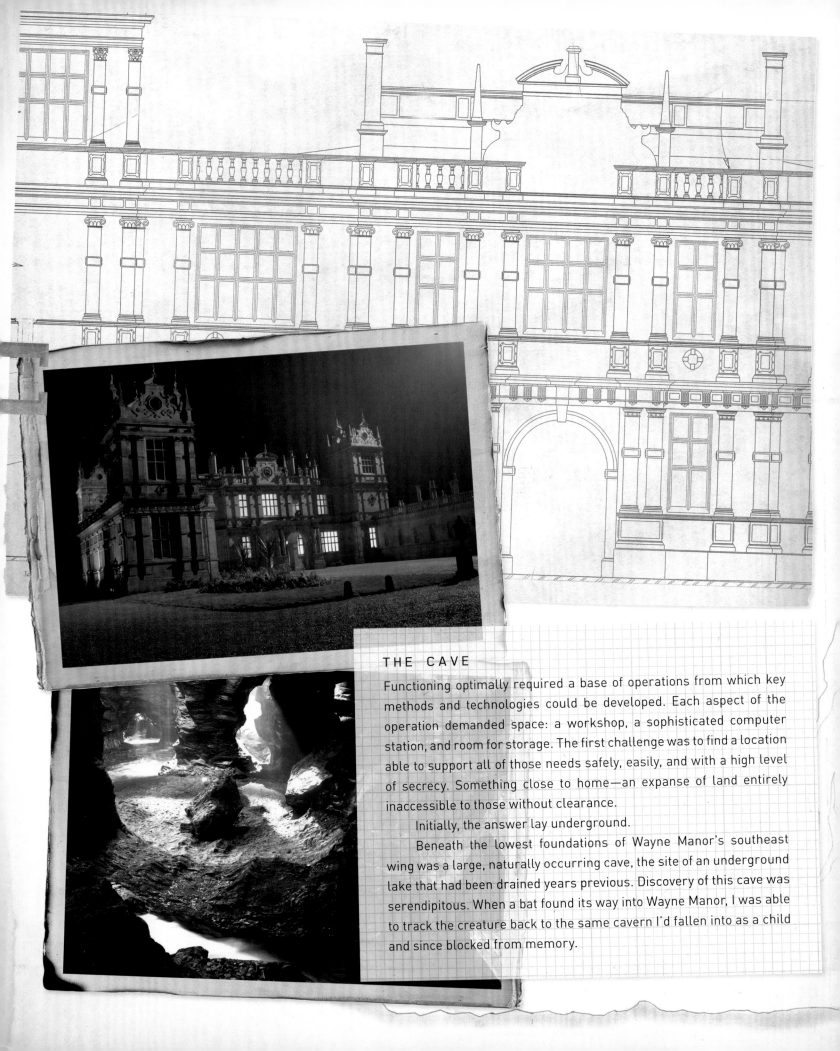

THE CAVE

Functioning optimally required a base of operations from which key methods and technologies could be developed. Each aspect of the operation demanded space: a workshop, a sophisticated computer station, and room for storage. The first challenge was to find a location able to support all of those needs safely, easily, and with a high level of secrecy. Something close to home—an expanse of land entirely inaccessible to those without clearance.

Initially, the answer lay underground.

Beneath the lowest foundations of Wayne Manor's southeast wing was a large, naturally occurring cave, the site of an underground lake that had been drained years previous. Discovery of this cave was serendipitous. When a bat found its way into Wayne Manor, I was able to track the creature back to the same cavern I'd fallen into as a child and since blocked from memory.

The terrain was damp, dark, and unpredictable, but the surrounding foundations were all durably built and well preserved; it had the potential to be exactly the space needed. Our first challenge was determining a contractor who could build this base without compromising the secrecy of the operation. The area was going to be a focal point in the war on crime, and no ordinary contractor could be hired to come in and create a war room out of a secret cavern. It became very clear that the space could only be transformed manually. There could be no construction crews, no earthmovers.

SECTION: BA-SE
PAGE: 17

CAVE DIMENSIONS

HEIGHT (MAIN LEVEL):	150'
LENGTH:	168' 2"
WIDTH:	122' 6"

CAVE CONTAINS HIDDEN OBELISKS THAT RISE AND SUBMERGE AS NEEDED FOR TRANSPORTATION LANDING.

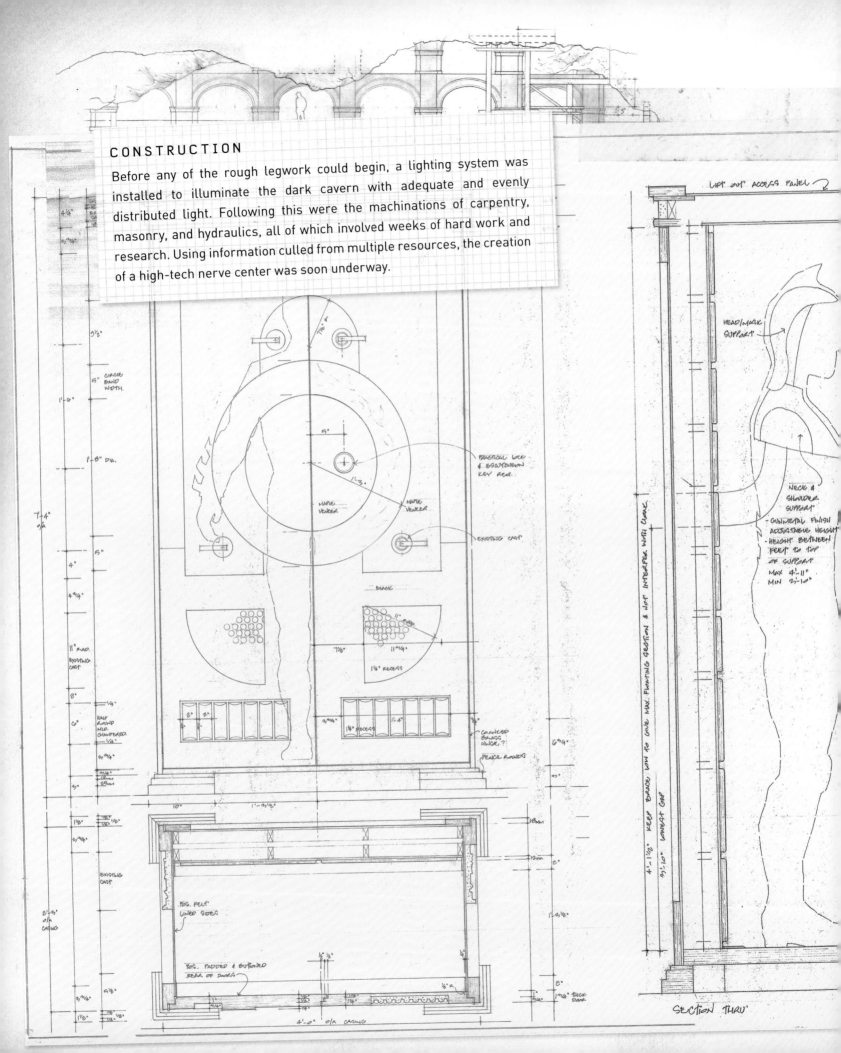

CONSTRUCTION

Before any of the rough legwork could begin, a lighting system was installed to illuminate the dark cavern with adequate and evenly distributed light. Following this were the machinations of carpentry, masonry, and hydraulics, all of which involved weeks of hard work and research. Using information culled from multiple resources, the creation of a high-tech nerve center was soon underway.

Originally, the cave sanctuary served as more of a workshop than anything else. Functionality took precedence over style. Several workstations were scattered around the cave, each catering to specific needs:

- A devoted space where weaponry could be taken apart and reassembled. Pieces of an arsenal could be improved upon after this type of reverse engineering.

- An area set aside to allow for the tailoring of the armored suit. Equipment included a battery-powered paint gun and an airlocked vault to shield the suit from accelerated deterioration.

- A protected space for beta testing any gadget augmentations.

- Safe storage for incendiary materials including explosives and volatile chemical agents.

- Emergency precautions, e.g., irrigation and evacuation protocols to preserve the headquarters' integrity in the event of explosion or fire.

- Surveillance of the manor grounds and external exits, controlled from a central-ized computer nerve center. This security system includes closed-circuit cameras to scan nearby roads for activity; audible and visual alerts to warn of intruders; ongoing scanning of police bands for activity and data; and protective storage for the mainframe computer.

BASE
19

REAR ELEVATION (PART)

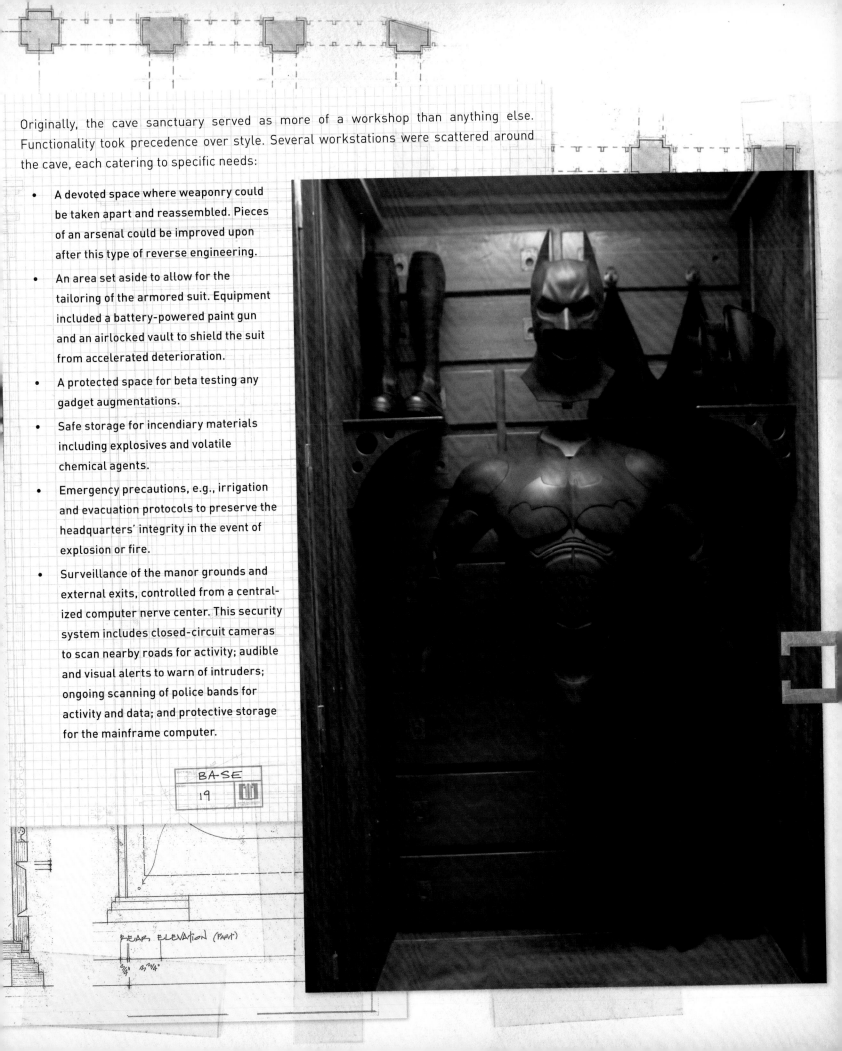

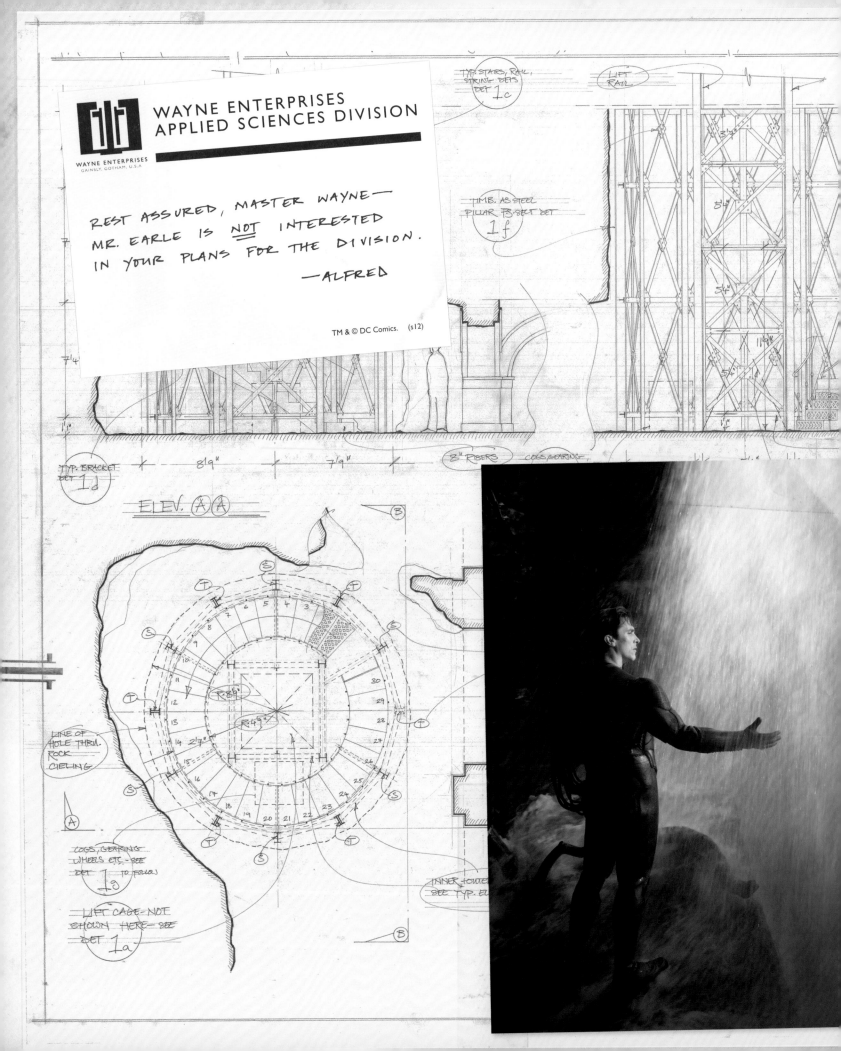

WAYNE ENTERPRISES
APPLIED SCIENCES DIVISION

WAYNE ENTERPRISES
GAINSLY, GOTHAM, U.S.A.

REST ASSURED, MASTER WAYNE—
MR. EARLE IS NOT INTERESTED
IN YOUR PLANS FOR THE DIVISION.
—ALFRED

TM & © DC Comics.   (s12)

9'4"

4

ACCESS

Direct accessibility to the cave was of utmost importance so that entering and exiting could be done quickly. The study within the Manor housed a piano on which a specific and muddled keystroke moved a panel in the bookcase to reveal a secret passageway. This corridor led directly to a freight elevator, which went directly down to the cave space.

Additionally, a discreet entrance on the underside of the property was separated from the outside by a crevasse and masked by a waterfall. What seemed unbreachable to the naked eye could be crossed in the Tumbler. Once inside, the vehicle was parked within the chamber in a crude, gravel-covered space, leaving enough room for it to enter and exit safely and securely.

BASE
21

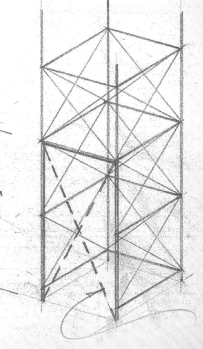

11'9"

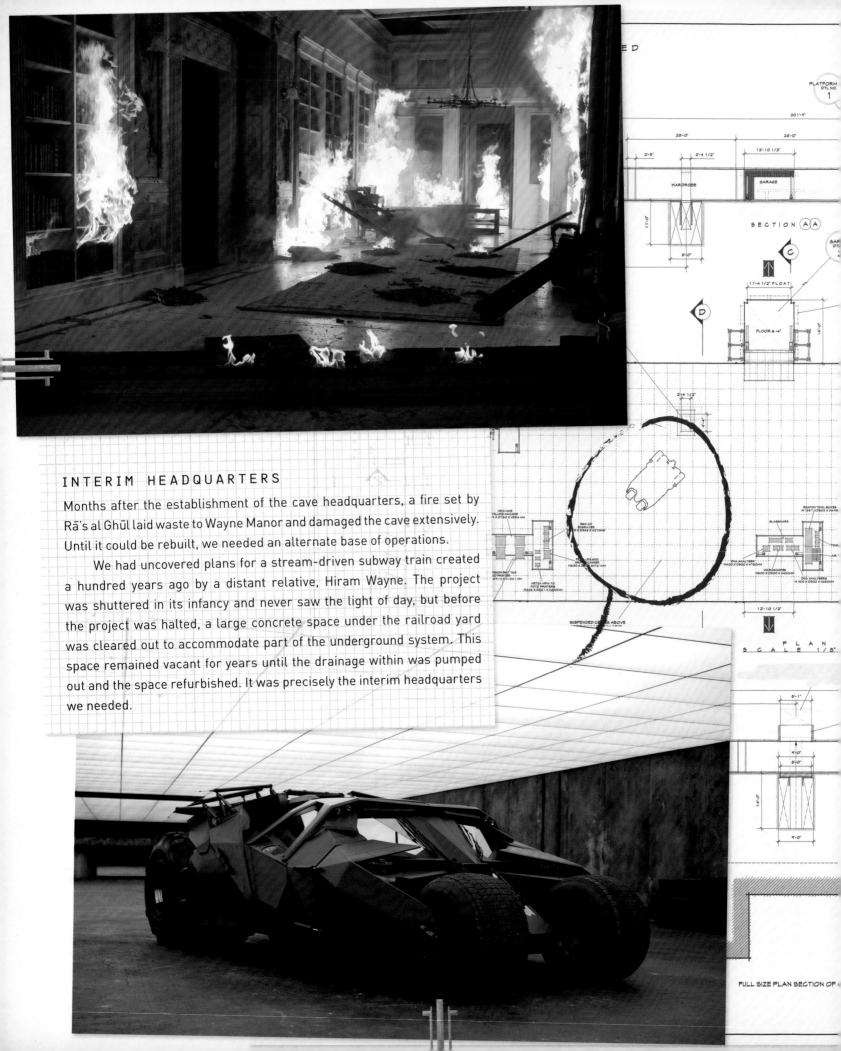

INTERIM HEADQUARTERS

Months after the establishment of the cave headquarters, a fire set by Rā's al Ghūl laid waste to Wayne Manor and damaged the cave extensively. Until it could be rebuilt, we needed an alternate base of operations.

We had uncovered plans for a stream-driven subway train created a hundred years ago by a distant relative, Hiram Wayne. The project was shuttered in its infancy and never saw the light of day, but before the project was halted, a large concrete space under the railroad yard was cleared out to accommodate part of the underground system. This space remained vacant for years until the drainage within was pumped out and the space refurbished. It was precisely the interim headquarters we needed.

This new "bunker" was more exposed to the outside world and raised concerns about security. Wayne Enterprises owned the rail yard above the bunker, but that didn't mean trespassers couldn't find their way in. The entrance was therefore kept very simple, in effect hiding in plain sight: a padlocked freight container housed an elevator that led down to the space. Movement in and out of the area had to be discreet. Security features were installed that would prevent unauthorized entry. Should an enemy make his or her way through the defenses when the bunker was unoccupied, each of the various workstations could lower itself into the ground, masking its existence. At most it would appear to be a vacant, well-lit parking structure.

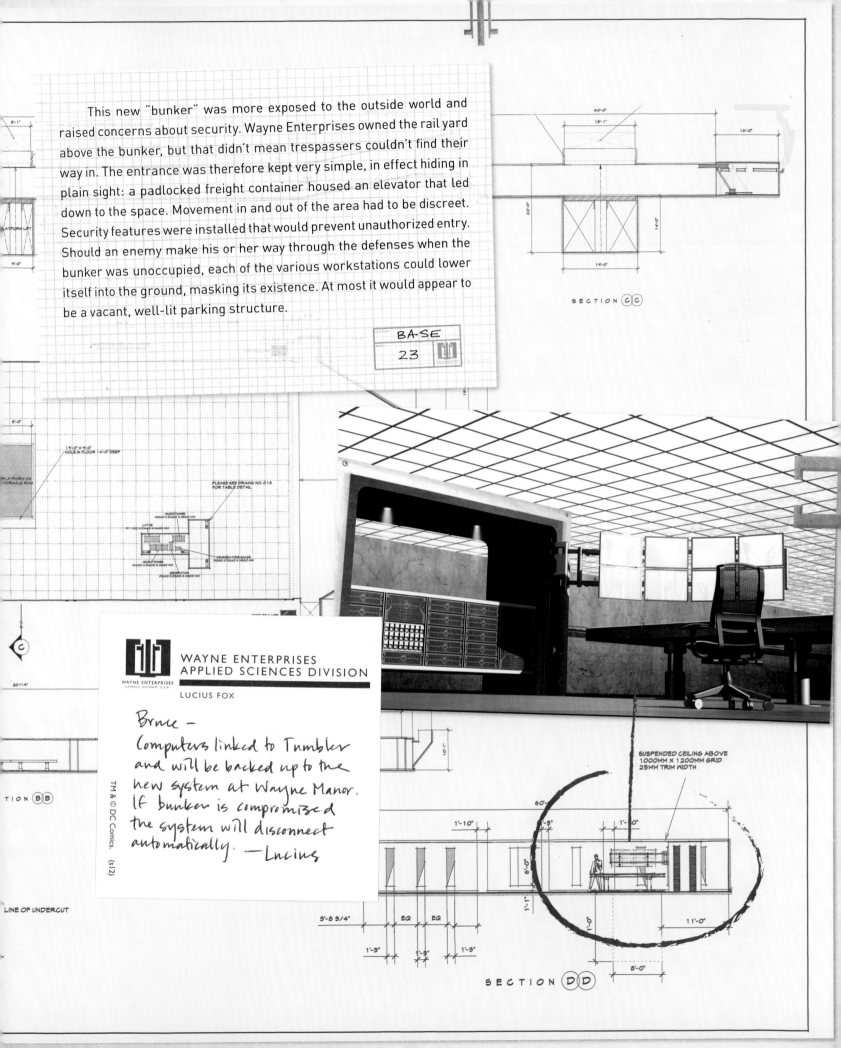

SECTION CC

BASE
23

WAYNE ENTERPRISES
APPLIED SCIENCES DIVISION

LUCIUS FOX

Bruce —
Computers linked to Tumbler and will be backed up to the new system at Wayne Manor. If bunker is compromised the system will disconnect automatically. —Lucius

SUSPENDED CEILING ABOVE
1000MM X 1200MM GRID
25MM TRIM WIDTH

PLEASE SEE DRAWG NO. 013
FOR TABLE DETAIL

LINE OF UNDERCUT

SECTION DD

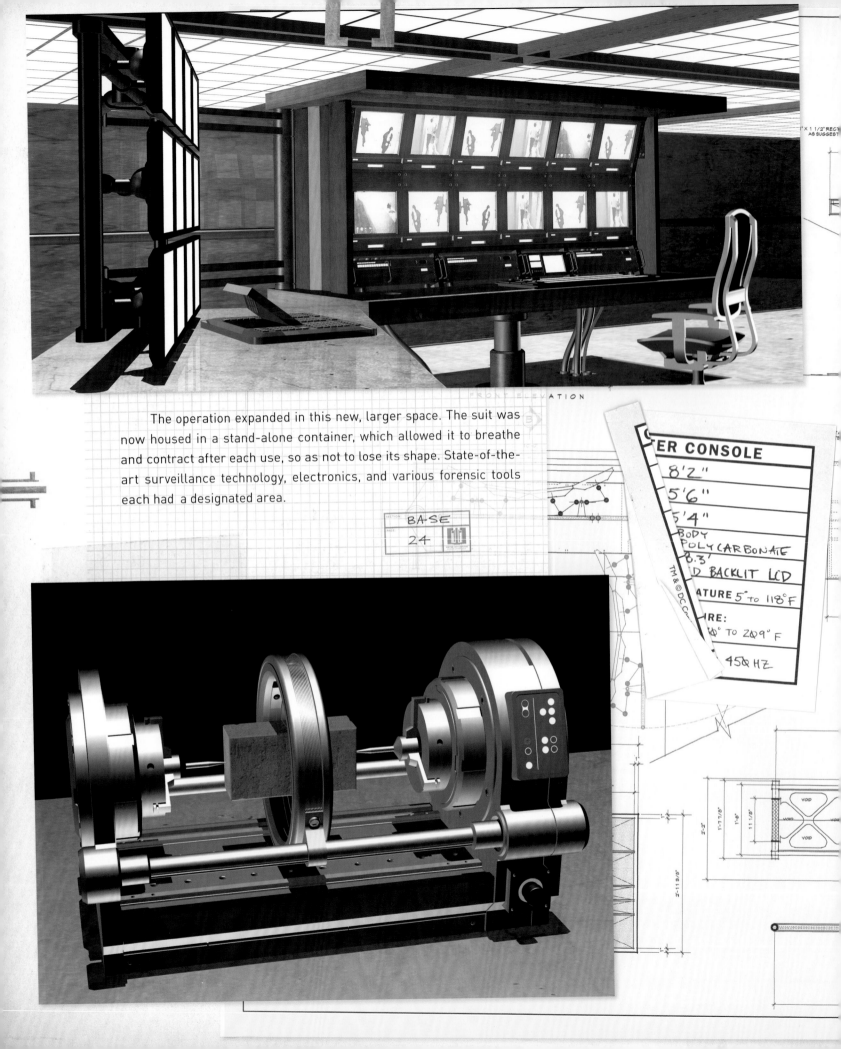

The operation expanded in this new, larger space. The suit was now housed in a stand-alone container, which allowed it to breathe and contract after each use, so as not to lose its shape. State-of-the-art surveillance technology, electronics, and various forensic tools each had a designated area.

SECTION BASE
PAGE 24

ER CONSOLE

8'2"

5'6"

5'4"

BODY
POLYCARBONATE
0.3'
D BACKLIT LCD

ATURE 5° TO 118°F

RE:

0° TO 209°F

450 HZ

CONSTRUCT

13'-0"

1'-0"

2 3/8" 1 7/8"
  5/8" 1" 2 7/8"

REAR ELEVATIO
ROOF PIECE SHOWN IN SECTIO

CTION WITHIN
PE ROOF

10'-0"

13'-0"

WORM'S EYE VIE

8'-11"

4'-6 3/4"

VOID   VOID

VOID   VOID   VOID

VOID   VOID

FRONT ELEVATION

PLAN
SCALE 1 1/2" - 1'-0"

4'-6 3/4"

8'-11"

THE CAVE REBORN

The success of the stripped-down bunker prompted the upgrade of the cave beneath Wayne Manor, with a renewed sense of proportion. It had begun as a much rawer space, and now could be streamlined, sparse, and transformable. The stone solitude of the bunker inspired the creation of a series of dark slate obelisks, which could rise and fall, thanks to a hydraulic system, depending on their specific needs. Each part of the new nerve center sat atop one of these massive slate cubes, making them all easily accessible. The movable stone slabs can also disappear into the ground, giving the impression—should outsiders approach—that it is merely an inactive, unremarkable cave.

Our surveillance equipment was expanded yet again, as were the database and streaming capabilities. Vehicle storage and readiness were crucial to the functionality of the cave. The Bat, an aircraft developed by Wayne Enterprises R&D, was recently added to the arsenal, and this flying vehicle is stored on a hydraulic stone slab as well. Bridges and ramps have also been constructed inside the cave, allowing freedom of movement from one area to the next. These have proven quite helpful for transport of equipment.

THE BATSUIT

THE SYMBOL

TM & © DC Comics. (s12)

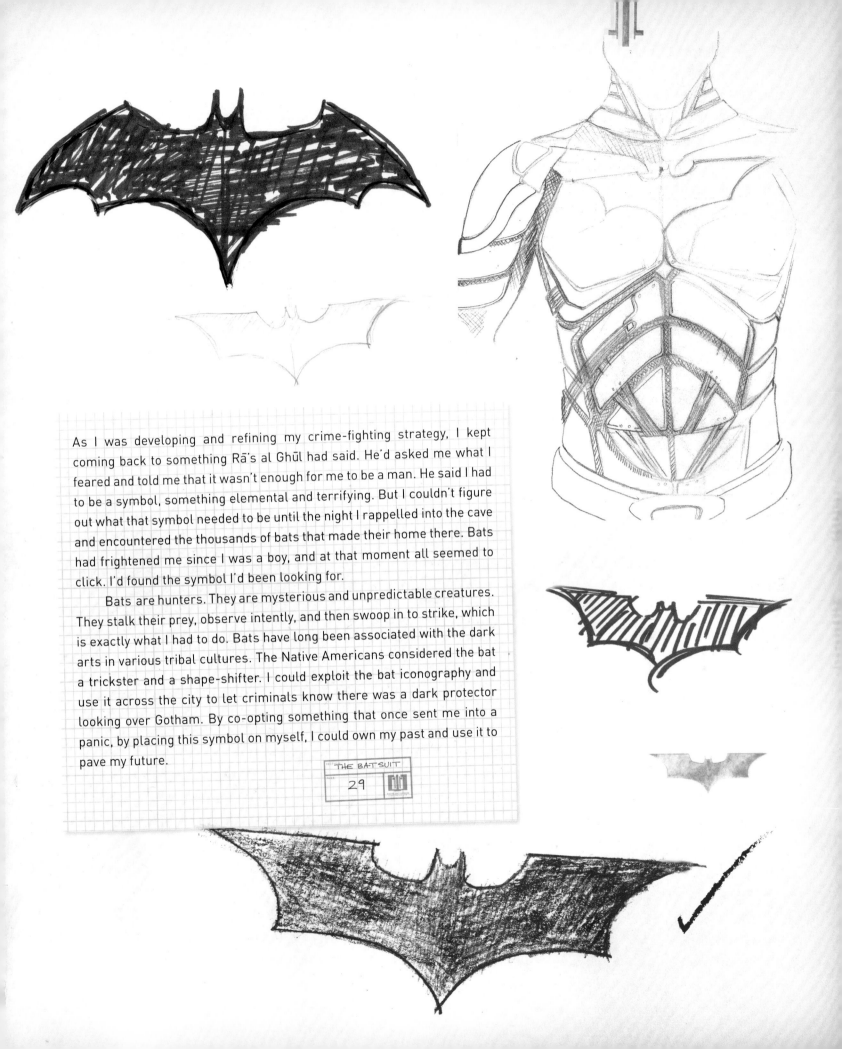

As I was developing and refining my crime-fighting strategy, I kept coming back to something Rā's al Ghūl had said. He'd asked me what I feared and told me that it wasn't enough for me to be a man. He said I had to be a symbol, something elemental and terrifying. But I couldn't figure out what that symbol needed to be until the night I rappelled into the cave and encountered the thousands of bats that made their home there. Bats had frightened me since I was a boy, and at that moment all seemed to click. I'd found the symbol I'd been looking for.

Bats are hunters. They are mysterious and unpredictable creatures. They stalk their prey, observe intently, and then swoop in to strike, which is exactly what I had to do. Bats have long been associated with the dark arts in various tribal cultures. The Native Americans considered the bat a trickster and a shape-shifter. I could exploit the bat iconography and use it across the city to let criminals know there was a dark protector looking over Gotham. By co-opting something that once sent me into a panic, by placing this symbol on myself, I could own my past and use it to pave my future.

THE BAT SUIT

29

THE BAT-SIGNAL

Publicly symbolic displays are an imperative part of maintaining a widely feared public persona. After Carmine Falcone was deposed from his perch atop Gotham's underworld, I strung him up in the shape of a bat on a searchlight. This sent the scum of the city a message that the Batman had taken him down.

This "bat" fashioned out of Falcone made its intended impression on then-sergeant Jim Gordon, who took the idea and created a summoning beacon. This new searchlight, placed on the roof of Gotham Police Department headquarters, housed a steel-framed bat outline it could project into the sky. Gordon could use the signal to contact Batman, or he could use it as a warning device, letting criminals know they were being watched.

This implement signaled the beginning of a shift in Batman's relationship with the department. Further, it sent a message to the people of Gotham that there was hope in the night. They were being protected.

BATSUIT

A symbol is pointless without the means to back it up. To function as Batman, I needed armor—protection. A suit: something simple yet dynamic, evocative, and as strong and sophisticated as science would allow. Gotham is filled with lowlifes who don't hold their punches. Batman must create the illusion that he is faster, stronger, and more powerful—even otherworldly. Invulnerable. Then he must perform as such. The suit would have to do far more than shield against the elements; it would have to protect against the unknown.

PRESUIT

The first chest piece was an Applied Sciences creation: strong and stiff and originally designed for advanced infantry use. The chest plate was made of a fire-resistant material composed of meta-aramid fibers. When exposed to heat or open flame, the fibers carbonize and bond, becoming thicker and creating a protective barrier. This prevents the suit from igniting or melting and protects the wearer for up to several minutes. The presuit's base layer was made of a tear-resistant Kevlar bi-weave, which boasts unmatched tensile strength. The material deflects knife attacks and bullets shot outside point-blank range.

THE BAT-SUIT

PAGE 33

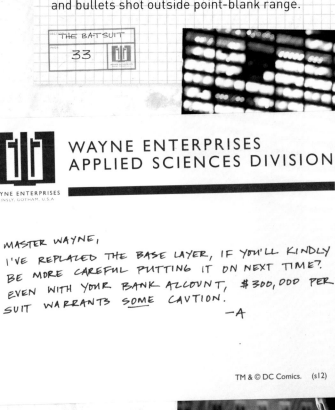

WAYNE ENTERPRISES
APPLIED SCIENCES DIVISION

WAYNE ENTERPRISES
GAINSLT, GOTHAM, U.S.A

MASTER WAYNE,
I'VE REPLACED THE BASE LAYER, IF YOU'LL KINDLY BE MORE CAREFUL PUTTING IT ON NEXT TIME?. EVEN WITH YOUR BANK ACCOUNT, $300,000 PER SUIT WARRANTS SOME CAUTION.
-A

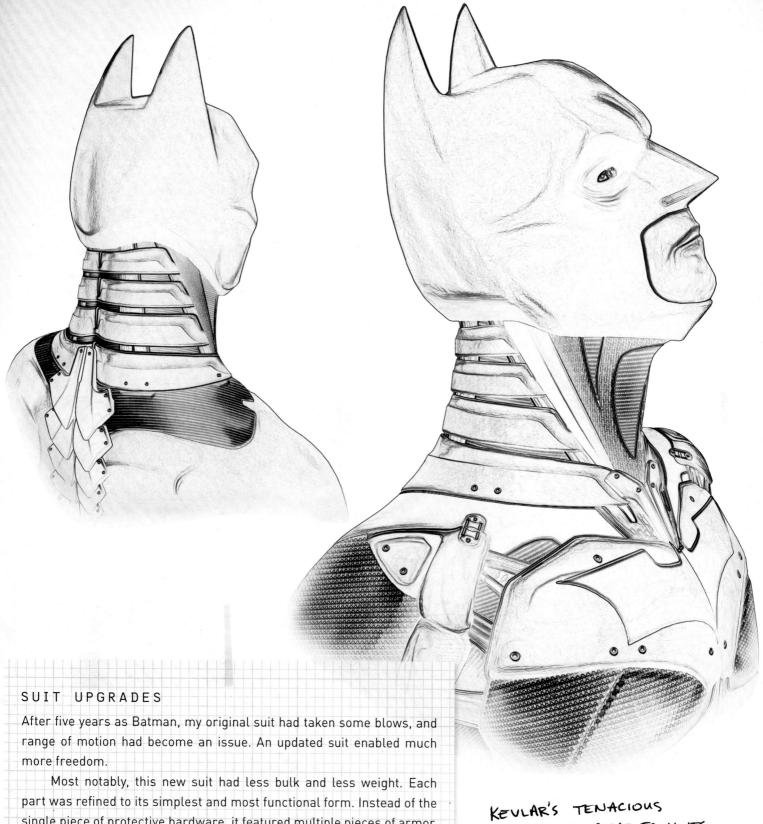

SUIT UPGRADES

After five years as Batman, my original suit had taken some blows, and range of motion had become an issue. An updated suit enabled much more freedom.

Most notably, this new suit had less bulk and less weight. Each part was refined to its simplest and most functional form. Instead of the single piece of protective hardware, it featured multiple pieces of armor, strategically placed and held together by a tri-weave elastic mesh. Hardened Kevlar plates exceeded all expectations, and the titanium-dipped mesh provided a crumple zone between the armored pieces, which gave me the ability to bend and twist without discomfort.

KEVLAR'S TENACIOUS PROPERTIES COME FROM ITS SYNTHETIC INTERWEAVE. FIVE TIMES STRONGER THAN STEEL. LIGHTWEIGHT YET FORMS AN EFFECTIVE SHIELD.

THE BATSUIT

34

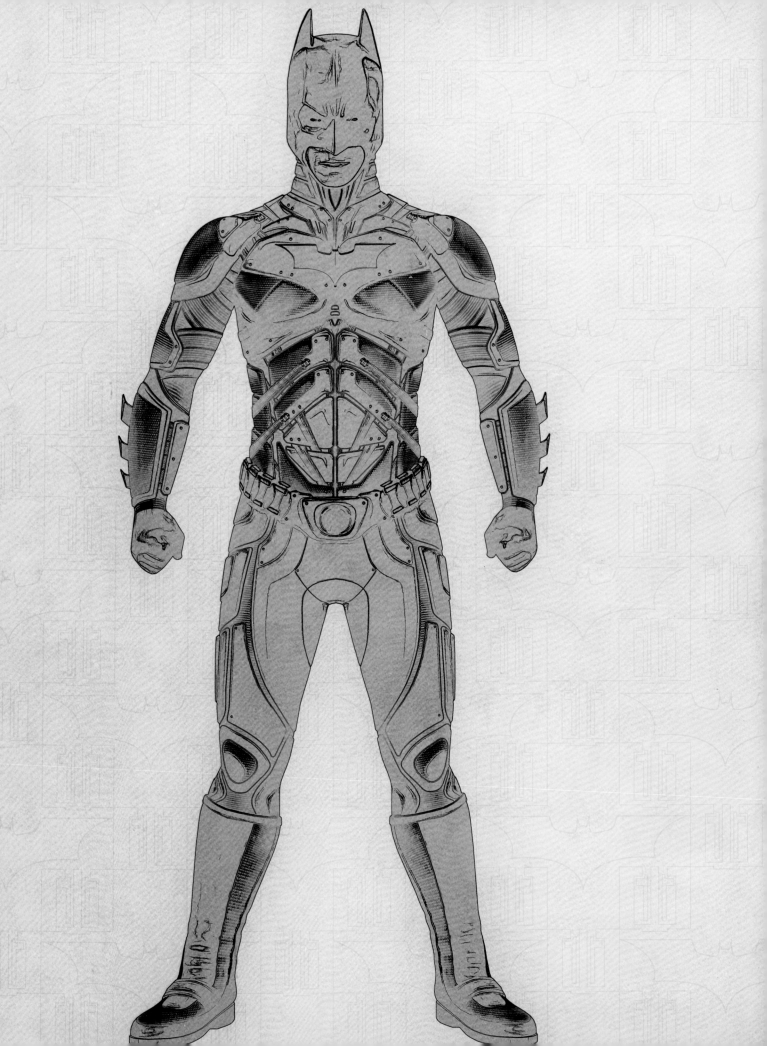

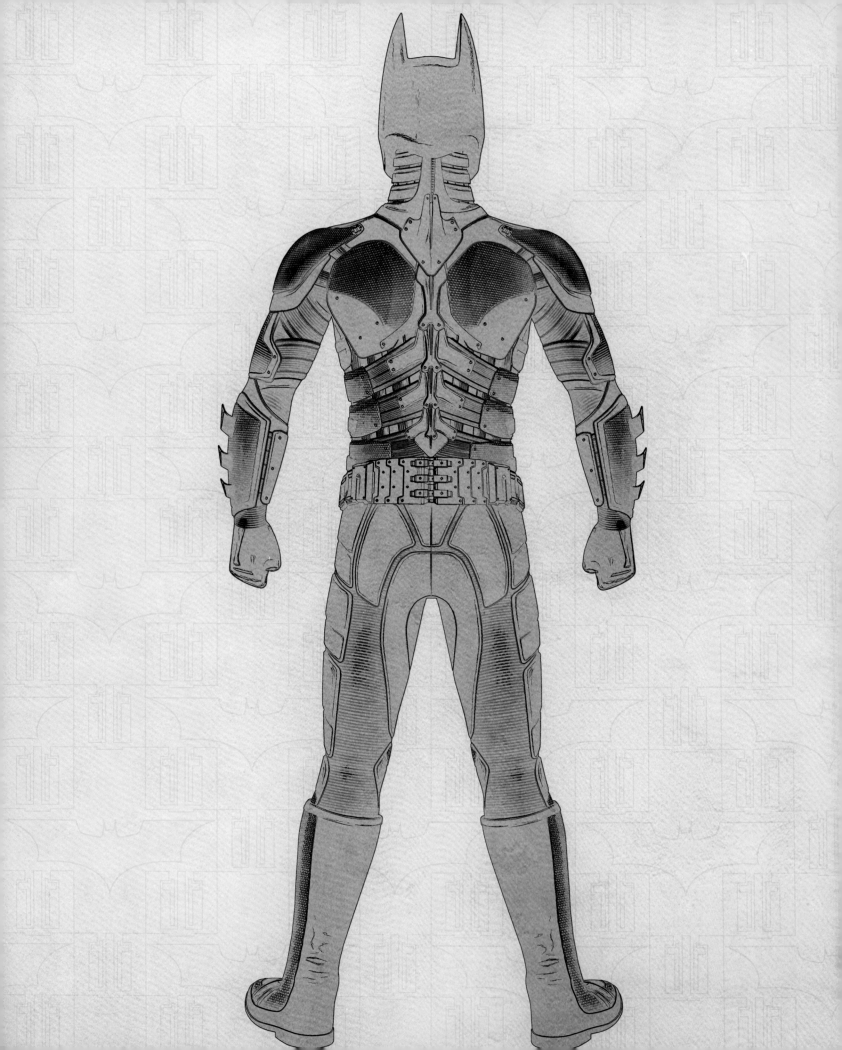

A smaller plating sequence around the midsection was designed to protect my core from direct attack. My previous cowl had prevented me from turning my head very far, so I divided the new head piece from the neck and made the neck piece part of my armored tunic. My vertebrae could rest and I could easily turn from side to side. Starlight night-vision lenses were also installed, which slid down quickly from inside the cowl and allowed me to see an attacker in the dark. Additionally, we added a new layer of storage to the back of the suit, which functioned similarly to that of a backpack. It was light in weight and easily stored my cape, packed flat, and allowed it to release when needed via a handheld controller during aerial maneuvers. All told there were 110 components to this new suit.

THE BAT-SUIT

39

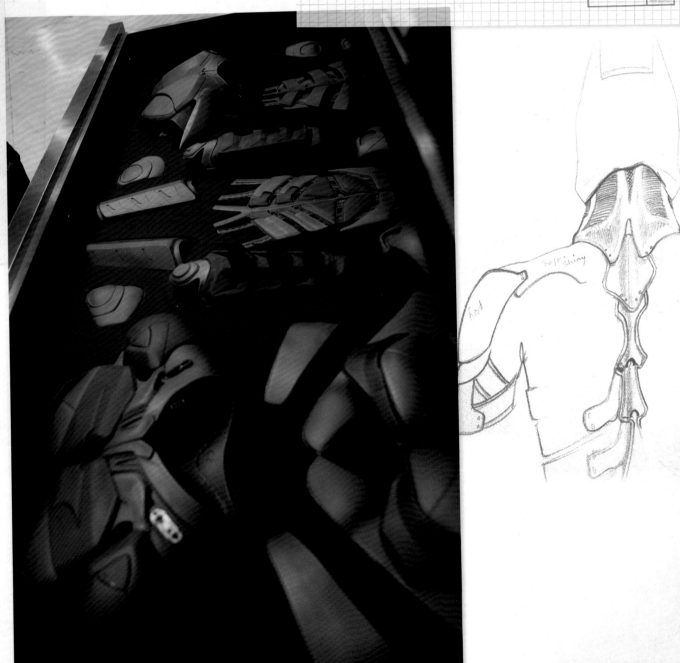

Soft shiny

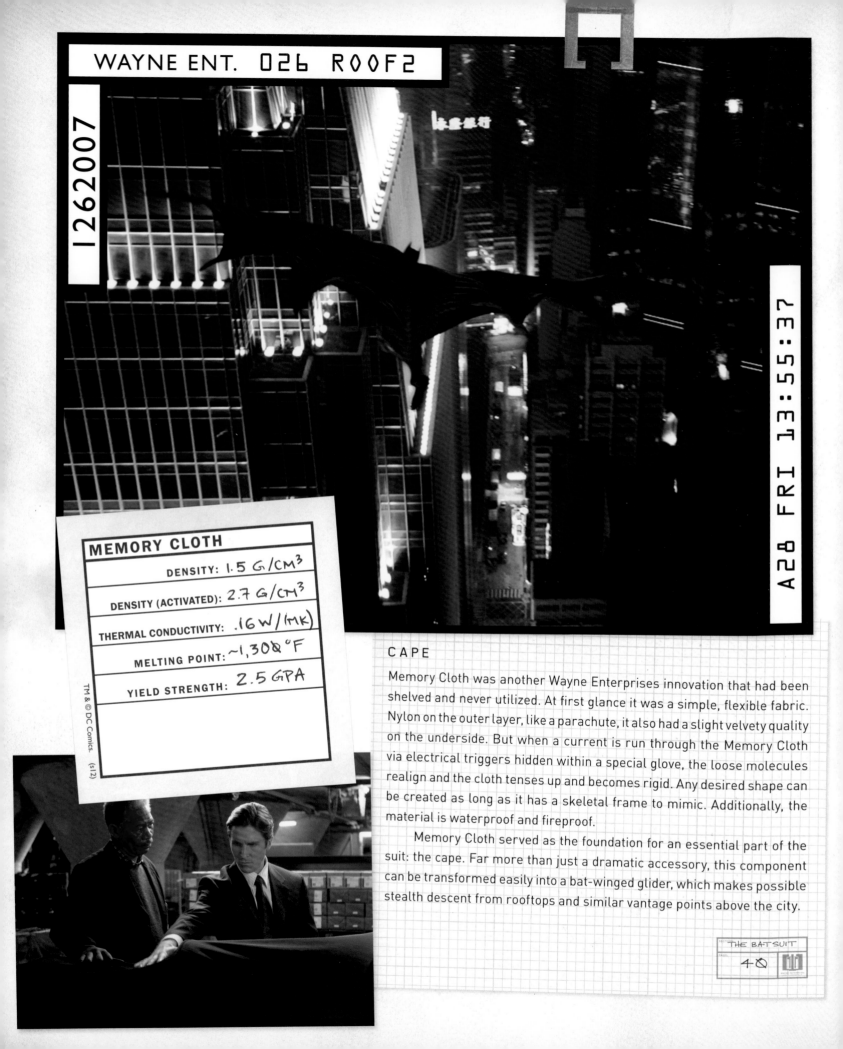

MEMORY CLOTH

DENSITY:	1.5 G/CM³
DENSITY (ACTIVATED):	2.7 G/CM³
THERMAL CONDUCTIVITY:	.16 W/(MK)
MELTING POINT:	~1,300°F
YIELD STRENGTH:	2.5 GPA

TM & © DC Comics. (s12)

CAPE

Memory Cloth was another Wayne Enterprises innovation that had been shelved and never utilized. At first glance it was a simple, flexible fabric. Nylon on the outer layer, like a parachute, it also had a slight velvety quality on the underside. But when a current is run through the Memory Cloth via electrical triggers hidden within a special glove, the loose molecules realign and the cloth tenses up and becomes rigid. Any desired shape can be created as long as it has a skeletal frame to mimic. Additionally, the material is waterproof and fireproof.

Memory Cloth served as the foundation for an essential part of the suit: the cape. Far more than just a dramatic accessory, this component can be transformed easily into a bat-winged glider, which makes possible stealth descent from rooftops and similar vantage points above the city.

THE BAT SUIT

48

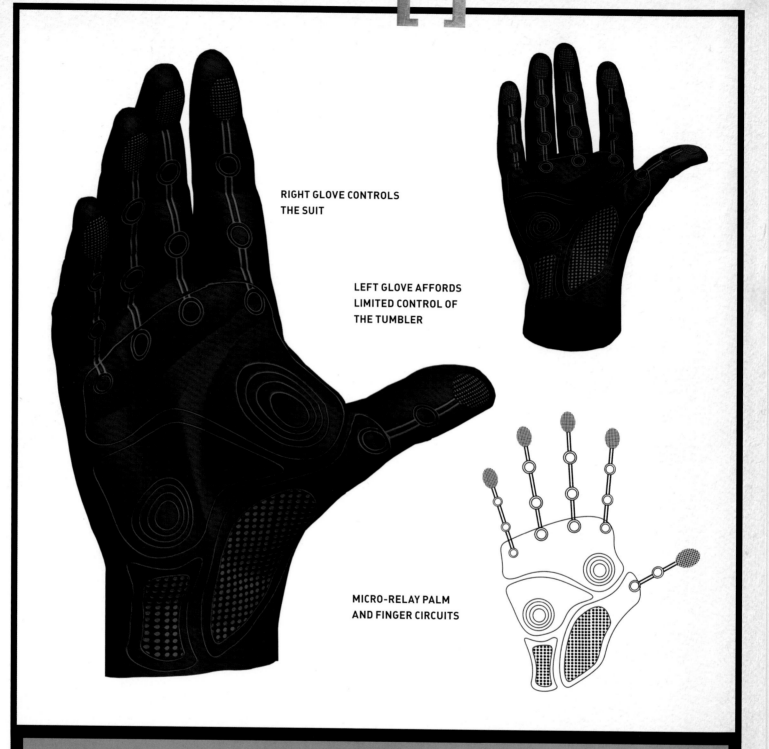

RIGHT GLOVE CONTROLS
THE SUIT

LEFT GLOVE AFFORDS
LIMITED CONTROL OF
THE TUMBLER

MICRO-RELAY PALM
AND FINGER CIRCUITS

BATSUIT GLOVES
CNT NO. JAG-112711 **PT. NO.** 3NE36W36

PROJECT NAME	CONTRACT NO.
BATSUIT GLOVES	PS23478
INTERNAL PROJECT NO.	SERIAL NO.
WF08642	LD-09-07

WAYNE ENTERPRISES APPLIED SCIENCES DIVISION

GAUNTLET 1.0

The scalloped bronze forearm gauntlets used during training with Rā's al Ghūl became a crucial part of the arsenal and were instrumental in repelling attacks. As noted, the gauntlets are perfect for blocking kicks and punches. Their jagged blades are a dangerous detail and something that lend the suit a dangerous-looking quality. For the Batsuit, the original gauntlets were modified with black latex paint, obscuring the ornate detailing, thereby making them more practical for urban warfare.

BLADES DETACH AS
THROWING STARS

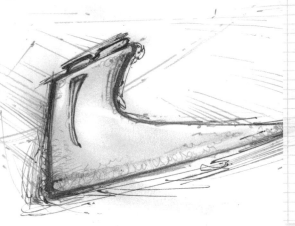

GAUNTLET 2.0

The next iteration of gauntlets elevated protection and deflection to new levels; opening up offensive possibilities. These gauntlets can be used for shielding as per usual, but jagged blading has become an optional feature—laying flat when in protective position and, with the touch of a button, extending in two rows of spikes. Further, they are now projectile.

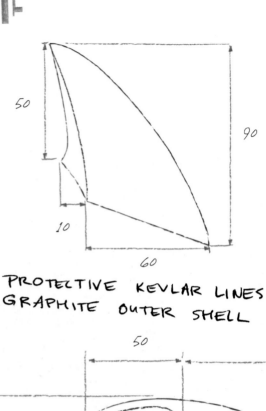

50

90

10

60

PROTECTIVE KEVLAR LINES GRAPHITE OUTER SHELL

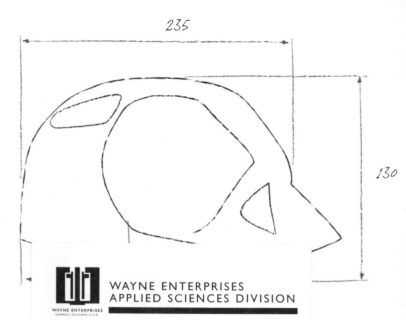

235

130

THE GRAPHITE ISSUE
HAS BEEN RESOLVED.
I AM PUTTING AWAY MY BAT
FOR THE TIME BEING.
        —ALFRED

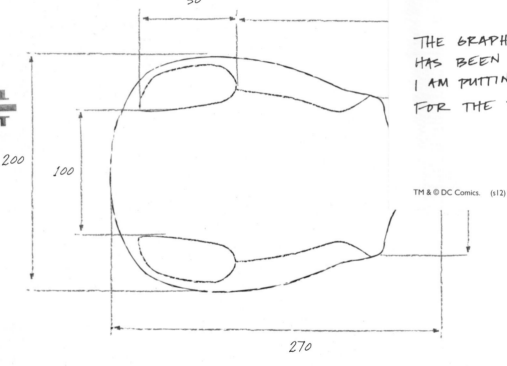

50

200

100

270

WEARER'S FEATURES ARE CONCEALED

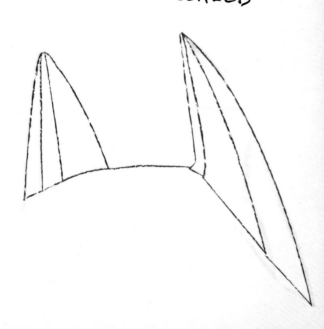

COWL

Hiding my identity was of the utmost importance, but I had to make it happen realistically while utilizing the theme of fear. A Wayne Enterprises impact-resistant headgear, developed for infantry, was modified with a faceplate that was specially ordered from overseas and made in bulk. Its graphite exterior housed Kevlar paneling, which made it impact resistant and protected the wearer from small-caliber firearms and concussive blows.

THE BAT-SUIT

44

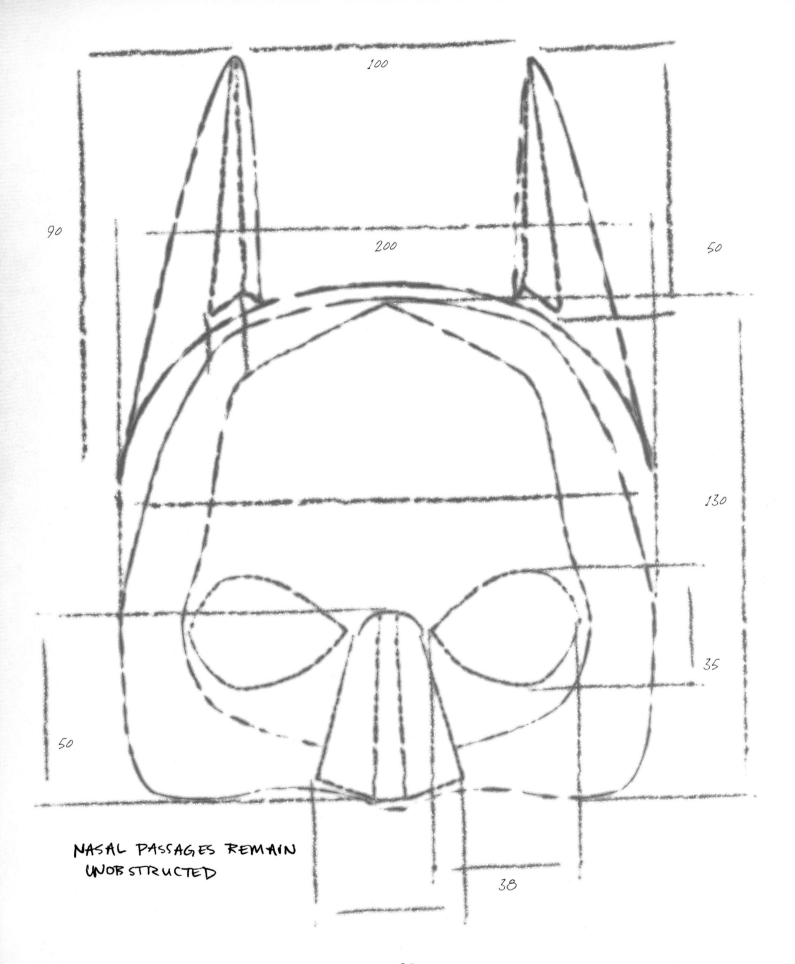

NASAL PASSAGES REMAIN
UNOBSTRUCTED

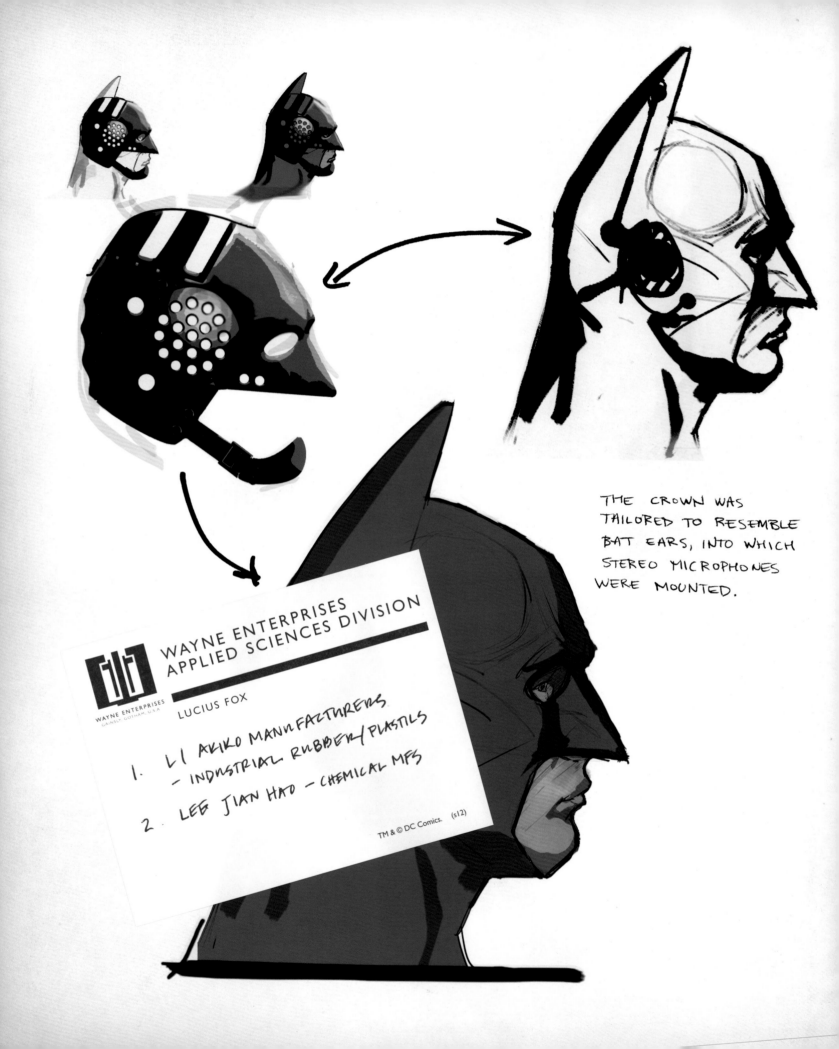

THE CROWN WAS
TAILORED TO RESEMBLE
BAT EARS, INTO WHICH
STEREO MICROPHONES
WERE MOUNTED.

WAYNE ENTERPRISES
APPLIED SCIENCES DIVISION

LUCIUS FOX

1. LI AKIKO MANUFACTURERS
   – INDUSTRIAL RUBBER/PLASTICS

2. LEE JIAN HAO – CHEMICAL MFS

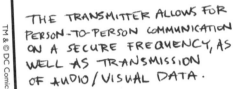

TRANSMITTER

CASE:	1MM POLYCARBONATE
WEIGHT:	0.82 OZ
DATA TRANSFER:	24 MBIT/S
FREQUENCY RANGE:	79 MHz

THE TRANSMITTER ALLOWS FOR PERSON-TO-PERSON COMMUNICATION ON A SECURE FREQUENCY, AS WELL AS TRANSMISSION OF AUDIO/VISUAL DATA.

MICROPHONE

SECTION

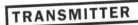

OUTER | | INNER

DIRECTIONAL MIKE

EARPIECE

PROTECTIVE COVER

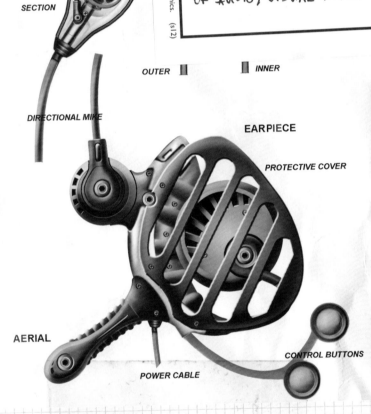

AERIAL

CONTROL BUTTONS

POWER CABLE

Over time the cowl's wiretapping capabilities were upgraded from short range to long range. We also improved security. Originally, four-part hidden snaps were used to protect my identity should I be knocked unconscious. I have since developed a device intended to produce an electrical shock, activated if anyone tried to remove the cowl externally. I added a system in the nose of the cowl, which filtered out harmful toxins and poison gases.

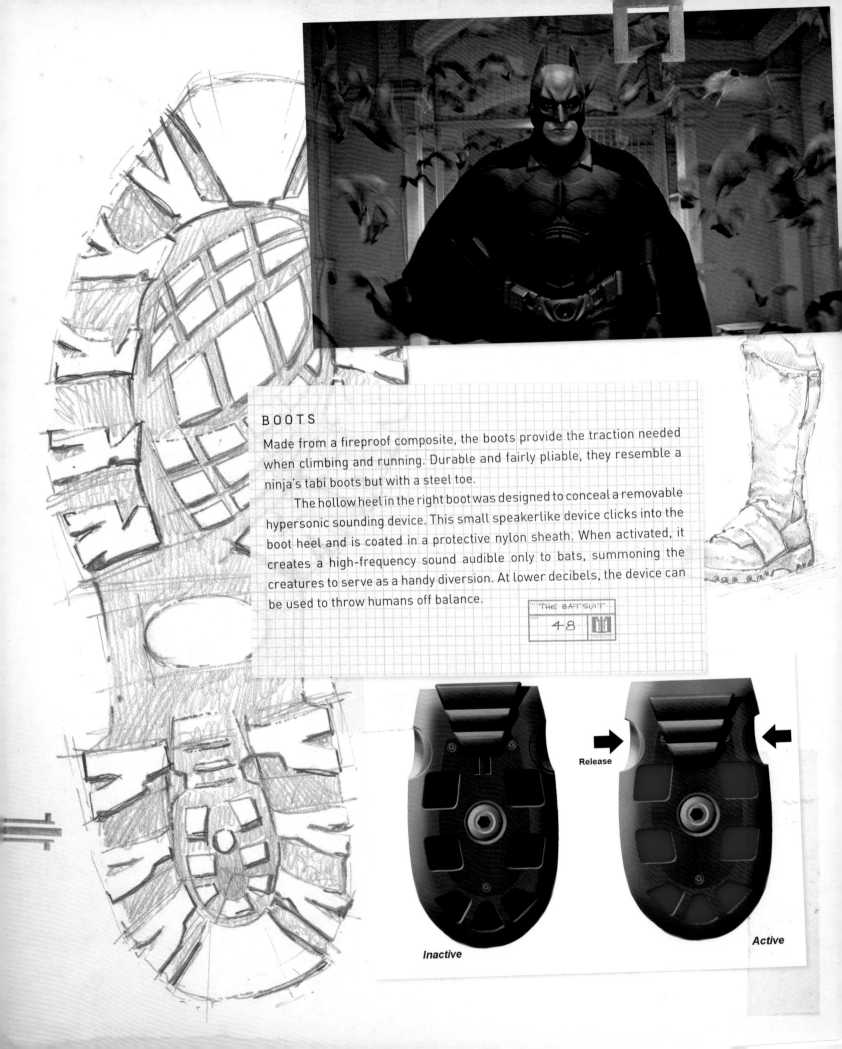

BOOTS

Made from a fireproof composite, the boots provide the traction needed when climbing and running. Durable and fairly pliable, they resemble a ninja's tabi boots but with a steel toe.

The hollow heel in the right boot was designed to conceal a removable hypersonic sounding device. This small speakerlike device clicks into the boot heel and is coated in a protective nylon sheath. When activated, it creates a high-frequency sound audible only to bats, summoning the creatures to serve as a handy diversion. At lower decibels, the device can be used to throw humans off balance.

THE BATSUIT

48

Release

Inactive

Active

DARK ARSENAL

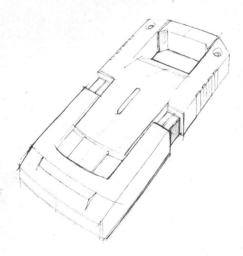

In the decades following my father's death, Wayne Enterprises was invested in becoming an arms manufacturer. However, under CEO William Earle, the pursuit of military technology was eventually deemed too costly and not lucrative enough, and Lucius Fox was charged with shuttering the company's various subsidiaries and consolidating assets so that they wouldn't fall into the wrong hands. This gave him intimate knowledge of—and access to—various highly advanced prototypes that could be co-opted for Batman.

Taking full advantage of these resources, an arsenal of highly functional and continually evolving weapons was developed to serve my needs. Firearms were not to be a part of this arsenal. After witnessing my parents being killed point blank by a gun, I swore never to use one or allow them to be used against those I cared for.

two part.

Lcd.

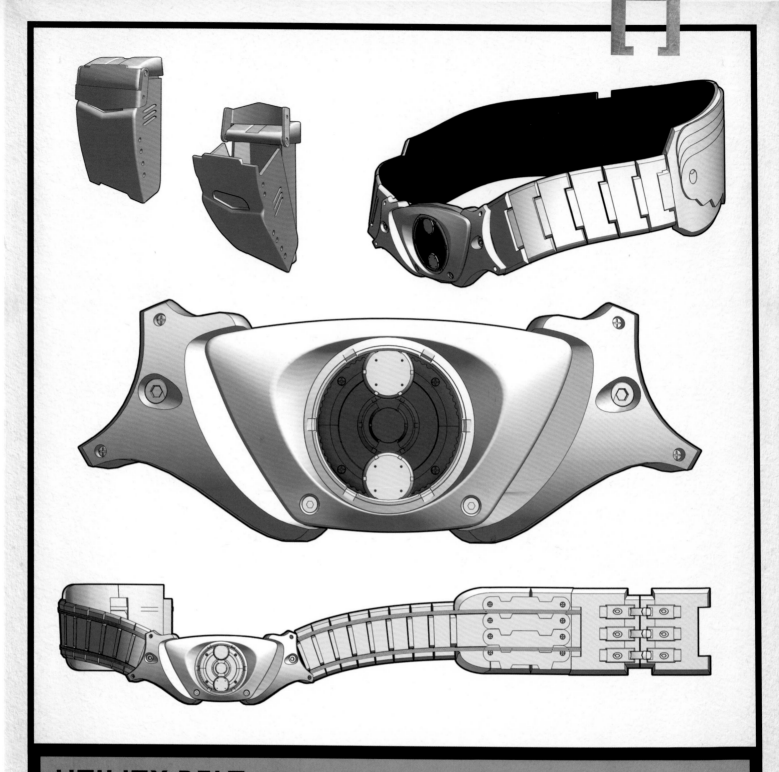

UTILITY BELT
CNT NO. RGK-093I **PT. NO.** 229-0640

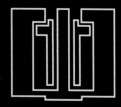

PROJECT NAME	CONTRACT NO.
UTILITY BELT	CT194772

INTERNAL PROJECT NO.	SERIAL NO.
YCSBK13478	STSR-09-13

WAYNE ENTERPRISES APPLIED SCIENCES DIVISION

UTILITY BELT

The utility belt is crucial, as it affords options. There is no Batman without it. Initially the belt was equipped with shoulder straps, which proved useless. Those were soon removed and the belt's shape and form were finalized. Its buckle features an easily rotating locking mechanism, to which various devices are attached. The belt itself was crafted from a titanium alloy and features a series of interlocking spring-loaded compartments to house various tools.

DARK ARSENAL
53

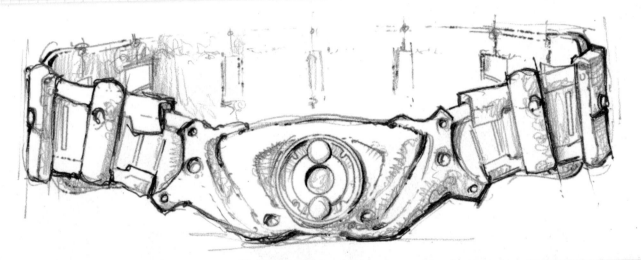

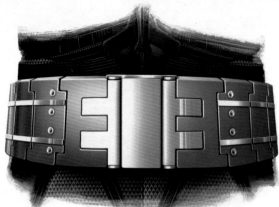

QUICK-RELEASE
BELT BUCKLE

SEGMENTED LINKS FOR EVEN
DISTRIBUTION OF WEIGHT.

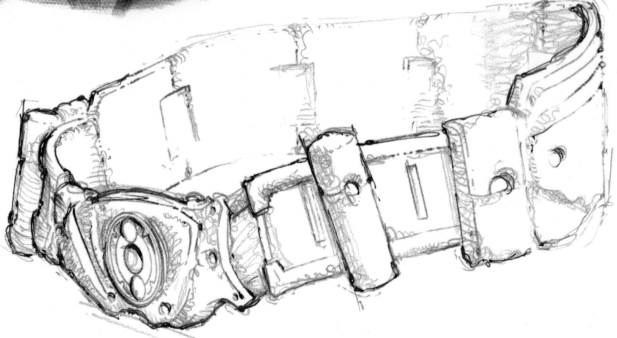

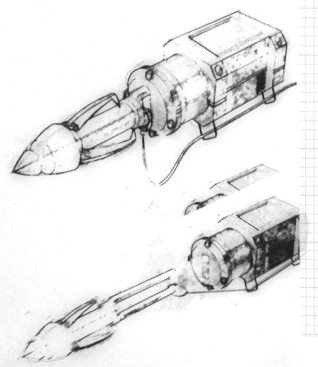

Among the devices housed on the belt:

- Emergency medi-pack

- Threat-specific remedies, e.g., injectable antidote to fear toxin

- Communication and tracking devices

- Assorted nonlethal deterrents; smoke bombs

- Ninja spikes for use in scaling vertical planes

- Grappling gun

Adaptations have been made as necessary. To accommodate larger devices, the back of the belt was enhanced with bracing that allowed the transportation of larger, heavier items without leaving them vulnerable to an opponent's grasp. To prevent the belt from falling into the wrong hands, it was made tamper-proof, wired for self-destruction should it ever become separated from the Batsuit in battle.

SURUDOI SAW

CNT NO. MNG-1014 **PT. NO.** JHG-091664

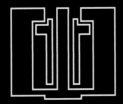

PROJECT NAME	CONTRACT NO.
SURUDOI SAW	68250229

INTERNAL PROJECT NO.	SERIAL NO.
KG-060578	11-11-96

WAYNE ENTERPRISES APPLIED SCIENCES DIVISION

TAMPER-RESISTANT LATCH

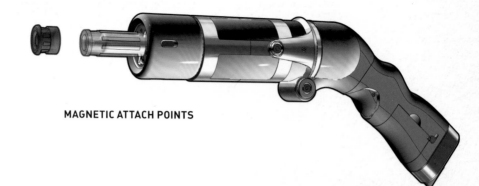

MAGNETIC ATTACH POINTS

ANTIDOTE AMPULES

BIO INJECTOR
CNT NO. GHJ-64169 **PT. NO.** NM-641410

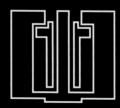

PROJECT NAME

BIO INJECTOR

INTERNAL PROJECT NO.

YGK-780506

CONTRACT NO.

11277889

SERIAL NO.

96-11-65

WAYNE ENTERPRISES APPLIED SCIENCES DIVISION

BATARANGS

Skilled use of a traditional throwing star (shuriken) can be an effective way to disarm and disorient criminals. Based on this concept, I fashioned a new kind of bladed weapon that Alfred took to calling a Batarang. Each one is made by hand, shaving down the metal pieces into a bat shape and fashioning them differently for each intended use. Each features a spring-loaded folding mechanism that makes them collapsible and easier to store in the utility belt. Because of its unique shape, the Batarang achieves a velocity greater than other throwable objects.

DARK ARSENAL

57

GRAPPLING GUN

Conceived as an all-purpose device that could fire projectiles for search and rescue as well as light combat, a Wayne Enterprises pneumatic grappling gun that used pressurized gas to create motion was the perfect device for my growing arsenal.

The gun works by shooting a thin monofilament wire with a magnetic hooklike grapple, which, when anchored to a sturdy object, can hoist humans as well as objects of great weight, with both speed and precision. In the field, it can be used in a variety of ways, but the simplest use remained that of a getaway device. The de-cel climbing line allows for rapid ascent and evacuation of an area with up to one other person in tow. Each wire coil cartridge fits easily into a storage pouch on the utility belt.

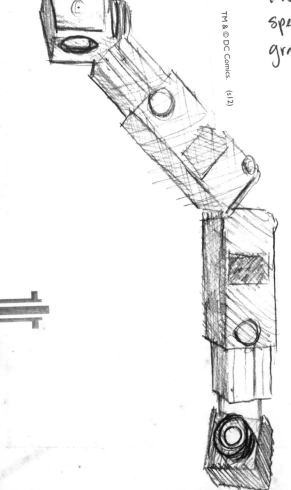

WAYNE ENTERPRISES
APPLIED SCIENCES DIVISION

LUCIUS FOX

Bruce –
I've enclosed the full specifications for the grappling gun.

TM & © DC Comics. (s12)

INFRARED PERISCOPE

Surveillance techniques are an evolving art form, and during a stakeout, an extendable infrared periscope remains an invaluable tool for on-site detective work. Infrared radiation produces a heat signature in a spectrum invisible to the human eye, but with a night-vision periscope, these heat signatures are illuminated, allowing the viewer to essentially see in the dark. Fiber optics create a total internal reflection and give the user the ability to look behind walls and around corners and a variety of other inaccessible locations.

The device's collapsible viewfinder also attaches neatly to the utility belt.

WAYNE ENTERPRISES
APPLIED SCIENCES DIVISION

MAGNETIC GRAPPLING GUN/HARNESS + BELT
CNT. NO. WE-679905 **PT. NO.** 235-3HK

WAYNE ENTERPRISES APPLIED SCIENCES DIVISION

PROJECT NAME

GRAPPLING GUN/HARNESS+BELT

INTERNAL PROJECT NO.

7568900-0966

CONTRACT NO.

WE-679905

48-G 2-PL

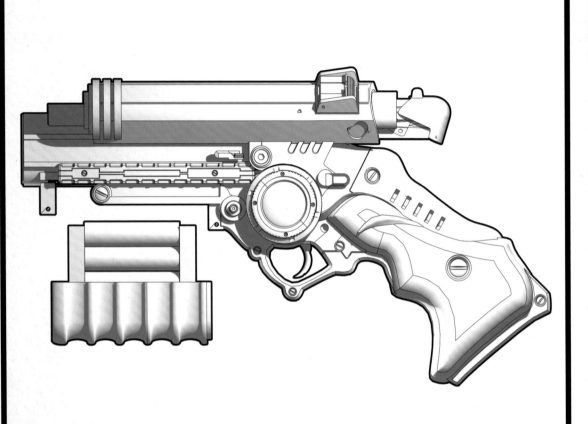

MAGNETIC GRAPPLING GUN
CNT. NO. WE-679905 **PT. NO.** 235-3HK

WAYNE ENTERPRISES APPLIED SCIENCES DIVISION

MAGNETIC GRAPPLING GUN

75689800-09GG

WE-679905

48-G 2-PL

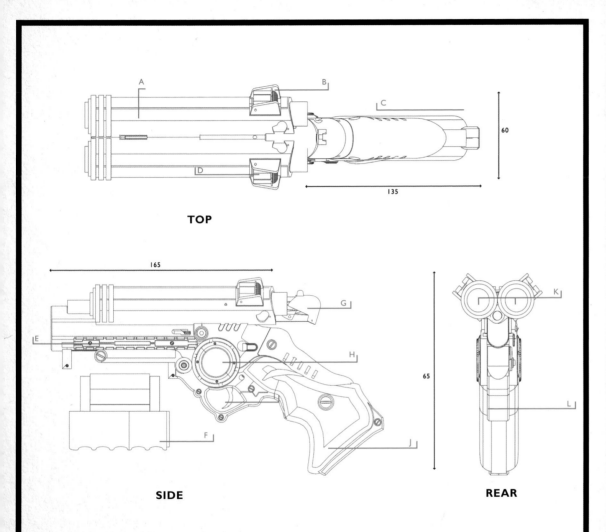

TOP

SIDE

REAR

MAGNETIC GRAPPLING GUN
CNT. NO. WE-679905 **PT. NO.** 235-3HK

WAYNE ENTERPRISES APPLIED SCIENCES DIVISION

MAGNETIC GRAPPLING GUN

756889800-09GG

WE-679905

TOP
A   TWIN BARREL
B/D   HIGH PERCUSSION
C   TRI-THOROID GRIP

SIDE
E   HYDRO RECOIL
F   GRAP RELEASE
G   GRAP RECOIL
H   ROTARY RETRACT
I   TRIGGER
J   TRI-THOROID GRIP

REAR
K   TWIN BARREL
L   GRAP COUNTER

48-G 2-PL

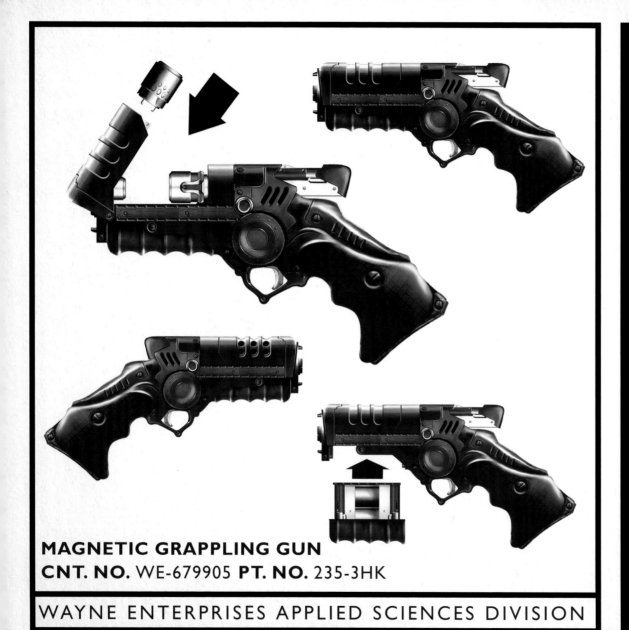

MAGNETIC GRAPPLING GUN
CNT. NO. WE-679905 **PT. NO.** 235-3HK

WAYNE ENTERPRISES APPLIED SCIENCES DIVISION

MAGNETIC GRAPPLING GUN

756889800-09GG

WE-679905

48-G 2-PL

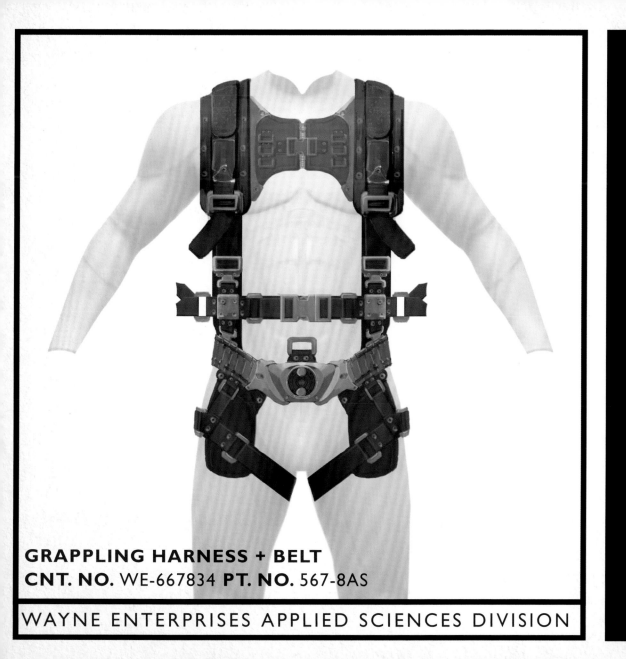

GRAPPLING HARNESS + BELT
CNT. NO. WE-667834 **PT. NO.** 567-8AS

WAYNE ENTERPRISES APPLIED SCIENCES DIVISION

GRAPPLING HARNESS+BELT

75690770-056GH

WE-667834

48-G 2-PL

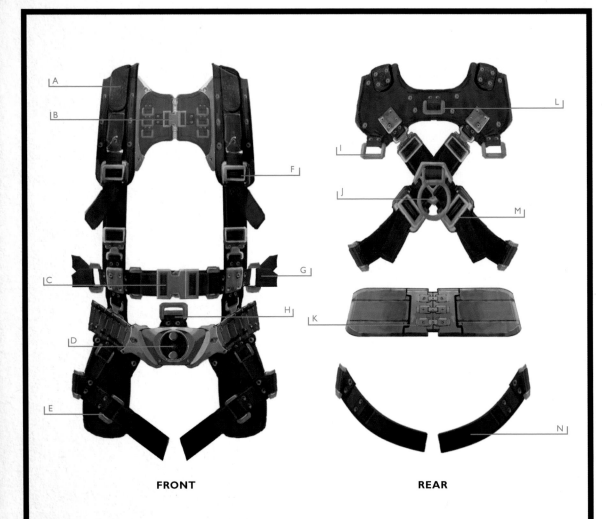

FRONT

REAR

GRAPPLING HARNESS + BELT
CNT. NO. WE-679905 **PT. NO.** 567-8AS

WAYNE ENTERPRISES APPLIED SCIENCES DIVISION

GRAPPLING HARNESS+BELT

756889800-09GG

WE-679905

FRONT
A   REINFORCED STRAP
B   ALLOY CHEST CLIP
C   ALLOY WAIST CLIP
D   ROTARY GATE
E   ALLOY THIGH CLIP
F   SELF-RELEASE STRAP
G   BENT-GATE CLIPS
H   BI-TOW STRAP

REAR
I   REAR BENT-GATES
J   REAR RELEASE
K   TRIDOG BONE BELT
L   PARACHUTE ATT.
M   ADJ. PLEX STRAP
N   RUBBER WEB STRAP

48-G 2-PL

INSTRUCTIONS FOR USE

1. ENSURE THAT CLIPS AND BELT STRAPS ARE ADJUSTED TO BODY SHAPE BEFORE USE.

2. THE TRIDOG BONE BELT SHOULD ALWAYS BE USED IN CONJUNCTION WITH THE HARNESS.

3. THE BELT BUCKLE CAN BE ADJUSTED USING THE ROTARY GATE (D). IMPORTANT: THE THREE-PIN MECHANISM MUST BE RELEASED BEFORE ROTATING GATE.

4. ENSURE THAT ALL JOINTS AND CLIPS ARE REGULARLY CLEANED WITH POLYPLEX SOLUTION TO MAINTAIN FLEXIBILITY AND PREVENT EROSION.

5. THE TRIDOG BONE BELT HAS BEEN DESIGNED FOR USE IN CONJUNCTION WITH THE MAGNETIC GRAPPLE GUN (MANUFACTURING PART NO. 235-3HK-K8) AND IS ATTACHED TO THE BUCKLE (D).

6. THE REAR-RELEASE MECHANISM (J) AND PARACHUTE ATTACHMENT (L) HAVE BEEN DESIGNED FOR USE IN CONJUNCTION WITH THE TRI-PLEXI FEATHERCHUTE.

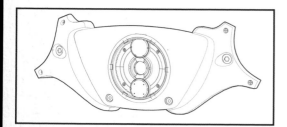

PRECAUTIONS

KEEP BARE SKIN AWAY FROM ALL MECHANISMS. ENSURE THAT HAIR IS SECURELY TIED BACK BEFORE USE. ALWAYS WEAR A SAFETY HELMET WHEN USING THIS HARNESS.

MANUFACTURE

The Grapple Harness + Belt have been designed for use in conjunction with the following mechanisms:

(Manufacturing Part No. 235-3HK)
(Manufacturing Part No. 985-9HP)
(Manufacturing Part No. 908-6JH)
(Manufacturing Part No. 208-4HP)
(Manufacturing Part No. 607-9BA)

All grips, fasteners and clips are adjustable and have been manufactured from 100% complex alloy and have been treated with Polyplex solution.

All straps have been constructed from rubber tubular webbing with advanced tensile weave, ensuring durability and flexibility.

All components of the Grappling Harness + Belt (Pt. No. 567-8AS) are:

TEAR-PROOF
100% BULLETPROOF
100% POLYPLEX FR IMPREGNATED
FLAME RETARDANT
WATERPROOF
THERMO TESTED

GRAPPLING HARNESS + BELT
CNT. NO. WE-667834 PT. NO. 567-8AS

WAYNE ENTERPRISES APPLIED SCIENCES DIVISION

GRAPPLING HARNESS+BELT

75690770-05GH

WE-667834

PATENT NOS.
5442264
5348728
5242682
5162501
5146218
5135911
3683810
3683812
3683813
3683819
3683836

48-G 2-PI

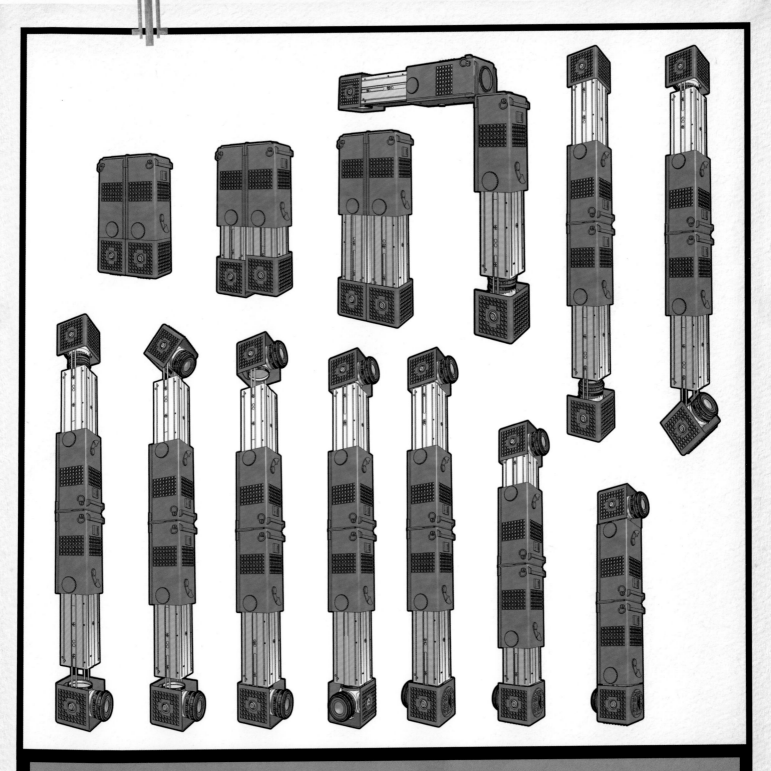

INFRARED PERISCOPE
CNT NO. KPG-111196 **PT. NO.** KYG-060598

PROJECT NAME	CONTRACT NO.
INFRARED PERISCOPE	10232011

INTERNAL PROJECT NO.	SERIAL NO.
MNG-10141964	09-166-4

WAYNE ENTERPRISES APPLIED SCIENCES DIVISION

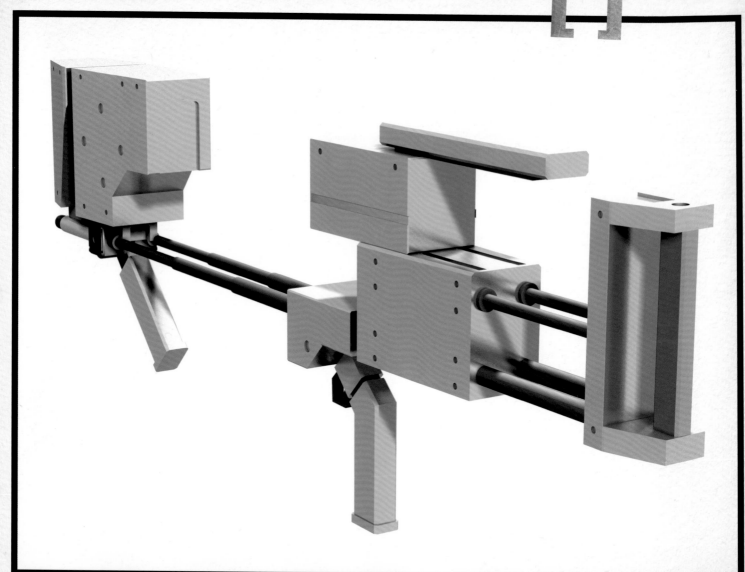

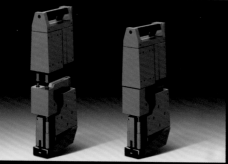

STICKY-BOMB GUN

CNT NO. HYO-121211 **PT. NO.** CS-R2000

PROJECT NAME

STICKY-BOMB GUN

CONTRACT NO.

6TXM460

INTERNAL PROJECT NO.

AW19784683

SERIAL NO.

BRC-03-01

WAYNE ENTERPRISES APPLIED SCIENCES DIVISION

STICKY-BOMB GUN

The sticky-bomb gun is a long-range, pump-action weapon used to fire timed explosives. These explosives, or "sticky bombs," contain an adhesive compound that allows them to attach to virtually any surface, with a range of over 100 feet. Embedded within the adhesive is a powerful explosive on a preprogrammed timer, which can be detonated at the user's discretion.

The gun itself comprises two halves, connected by two collapsible rods. A steadying device at the front of the gun ensures accuracy. After use, the gun can be folded into a compact, boxlike shape and stored on the back of the utility belt.

DARK ARSENAL
61

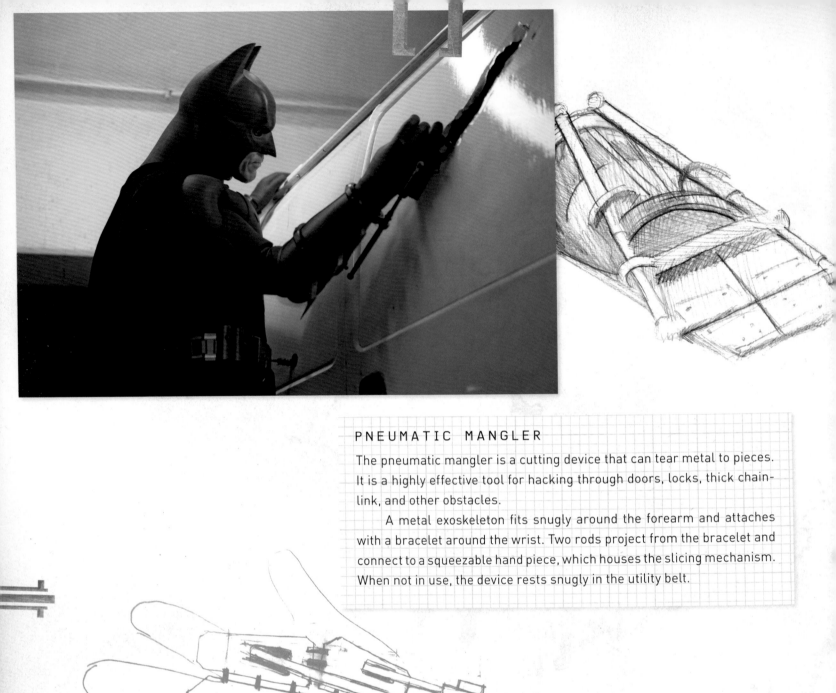

PNEUMATIC MANGLER

The pneumatic mangler is a cutting device that can tear metal to pieces. It is a highly effective tool for hacking through doors, locks, thick chain-link, and other obstacles.

A metal exoskeleton fits snugly around the forearm and attaches with a bracelet around the wrist. Two rods project from the bracelet and connect to a squeezable hand piece, which houses the slicing mechanism. When not in use, the device rests snugly in the utility belt.

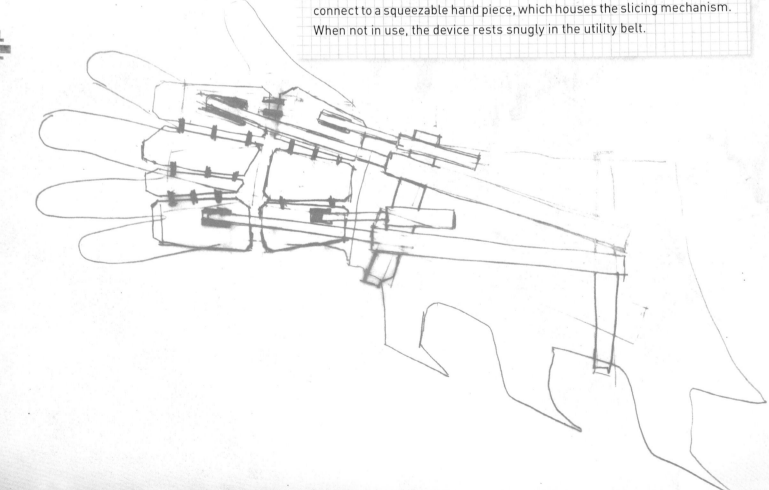

MINI-MINES

The mini-mine is a small, palm-sized bomb made up of thermite, a fine metal powder. Pressing a small button on the mine activates the release of magnesium, which when combined with the thermite causes it to combust. It works for a variety of purposes, but its genesis lies in diversionary tactics. Whether in hand-to-hand combat or battle involving artillery weaponry, a contained explosion and subsequent billow of smoke disorient the enemy's senses and produce anxiety, opening a window to strike and dismantle an attack.

Mini-mines also serve well as an offensive armament and are ideal for blasting through an impenetrable brick wall or thick steel door, enabling entry into otherwise locked locations.

In addition to explosive capabilities, a second version of the mini-mine features razor-sharp edges. This visually threatening weapon is capable of causing significant damage. Released from a vehicle in multiple, the mini-mine will facilitate escape from a chase situation.

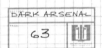

DARK ARSENAL

63

FROM THE DESK OF
BRUCE WAYNE

These were developed as a diversionary device but you may find them more useful as a skeleton key of sorts.

—Lucius

WE FIRST BECAME AWARE OF THE THREAT POSED BY HONG KONG-BASED ACCOUNTING FIRM L.S.I. HOLDINGS WHEN OUR SYSTEM REPORTED SUSPICIOUS TRANSACTIONS MADE BY ITS CHIEF ACCOUNTANT. LAU'S ALLEGED TIES TO THE MOB SOON BECAME PUBLIC. HE FLED BACK TO HONG KONG WHERE HE COULDN'T BE EXTRADITED AS A CHINESE NATIONAL. THE SKYHOOK MISSION WAS LAUNCHED IN ORDER TO RETURN LAU TO GOTHAM FOR PROSECUTION.

SKYHOOK

Skyhook, a surface-to-air recovery system, has been used for years by various military agencies around the world. The operation is designed to rescue ground combatants from enemy hot spots during their time of need. A subject must strap into a harness while simultaneously releasing a small self-inflated helium balloon attached to a braided nylon lift line. The other end of the line is securely fastened to the harness. Timed to coincide with the balloon's release, a support aircraft is sent into the pickup zone, where indicator lights on the lift line help guide the pilot toward the retrieval subject. As the aircraft passes it catches the lift line and scoops up the subjects, reeling them into the back of the plane in the process. For the mission to capture Lau, a former navy cargo ship was acquired and a flight crew of South Korean smugglers were found to pilot it.

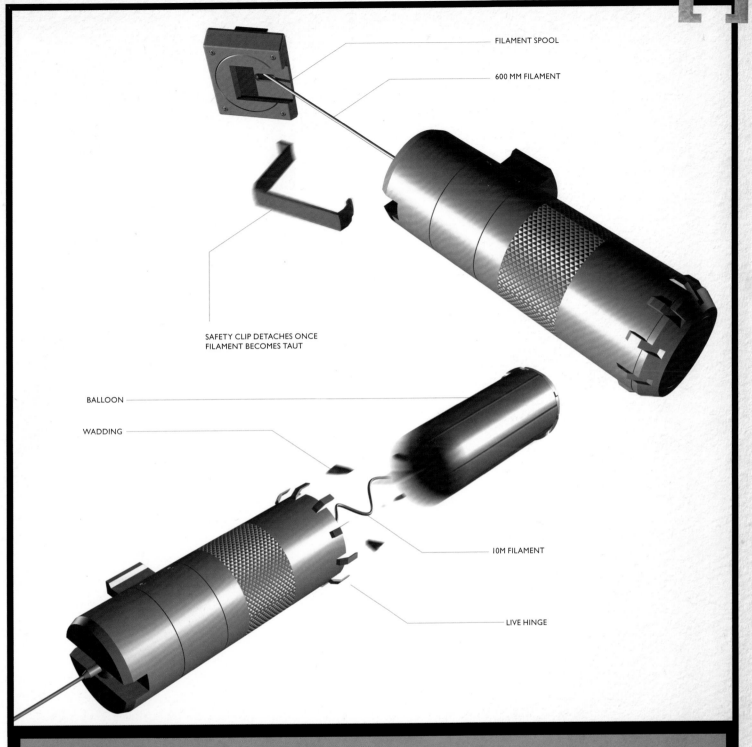

FILAMENT SPOOL

600 MM FILAMENT

SAFETY CLIP DETACHES ONCE
FILAMENT BECOMES TAUT

BALLOON

WADDING

10M FILAMENT

LIVE HINGE

SKYHOOK

CNT NO. HYO-10001 **PT. NO.** HANA-06404

PROJECT NAME	CONTRACT NO.
SKYHOOK	IE10P0012

INTERNAL PROJECT NO.	SERIAL NO.
TOB320216	98-11-14

WAYNE ENTERPRISES APPLIED SCIENCES DIVISION

SONAR PROJECT

Lucius Fox created a small sonar device that was able to chart an environment using sound waves. Essentially this device mimics the natural abilities of a bat and the man-made abilities of a submarine. The basic electronic mechanism is similar to that of a cellular phone. When placed in a secure location, the device sends out an inaudible frequency that records response times and then uses those signals to map an area. These maps can then be combined to form a complete visual image. In keeping with the idea of using surveillance technology as an active part of field operations, the original sonar device has been modified to enhance its capabilities and give it much wider range. It also acts as a high-frequency receiver microphone that can emit a visual image of its surroundings. These images are then broadcast to a bank of monitors located in the Wayne Enterprises building.

Enhancements have been made to the Batsuit to allow for mobile utilization of sonar through special lenses in the cowl. As needed, the lenses slide down to cover the eye area and feed images in real time. Because of the breadth and scope of our operation, the monitor bay must be manned in order to feed direction in the field and triangulate positioning. The monitor unit features a database encryption, which means it is only accessible by one person: Lucius Fox. Further, a unique self-destruct system was built into the device. Upon completion of the operation, Fox simply types his name into the unit and it self-destructs.

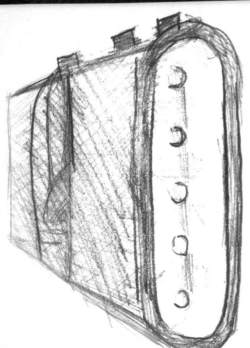

EMP DEVICE

In order to effect a communications blackout, a device is used that delivers an electromagnetic pulse that can disrupt electronic equipment. The pulse is able to activate and deactivate at a preset time for the requested length needed. This gadget effectively cancels all closed-circuit camera feeds as well as cellular transmissions, within a predetermined distance. It must, however, be within close proximity of the area that it is affecting in order to remain effective.

MICROWAVE EMITTER

The Wayne Enterprises 47B1 Microwave Emitter was a device intended for altruistic purposes but was co-opted by Rā's al Ghūl in his efforts to destroy Gotham City. This experimental prototype was originally created for desert warfare and, when functional, could focus the power of microwaves to vaporize an enemy's water supply. In the arid desert, this kind of attack can cripple a fighting force. The device was also capable of dispersing water-based chemical agents, which was its intended use under Rā's direction. The Scarecrow's fear toxin was given a liquid form and fed directly into the city's water system, where it lay in wait for the emitter's activation. The microwave emitter was then loaded onto Gotham's monorail system and positioned on a moving train headed straight for the center of town, where the city's water and power utilities converged at the heart of Wayne Tower. Travelling quickly along the track as it passed through the city, the mechanism mobilized and the central dispersal unit transformed the city's water supply into paralyzing fear gas. At the same time, the toxin's quick transformation from water to gas caused incredible pressure to build, which threatened to destroy entire sections of the city.

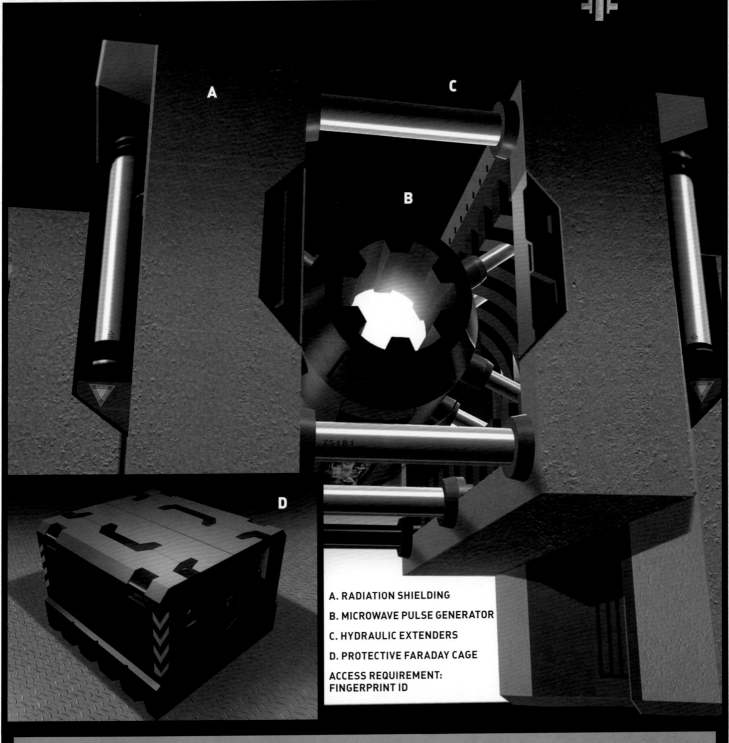

A. RADIATION SHIELDING

B. MICROWAVE PULSE GENERATOR

C. HYDRAULIC EXTENDERS

D. PROTECTIVE FARADAY CAGE

ACCESS REQUIREMENT:
FINGERPRINT ID

MICROWAVE EMITTER
CNT NO. MHG093001 **PT. NO.** 229-1935

PROJECT NAME
MICROWAVE EMITTER

CONTRACT NO.
FCT197463

INTERNAL PROJECT NO.
YCSBK1662

SERIAL NO.
BFD-09-16

WAYNE ENTERPRISES APPLIED SCIENCES DIVISION

VEHICLES

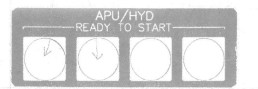
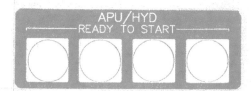

THE TUMBLER

Quick and efficient travel within Gotham was an operational priority. I needed something modern and sophisticated—a strong utility vehicle with the speed and grace of a sports car—able to move in and out of the city without being tracked. As a symbol of the night, Batman needed transportation that matched his fearful persona but that was also multifunctional, extremely well fortified, and equipped with weaponry that could take out inorganic obstacles.

The Tumbler was originally built as a military bridging vehicle that could transport soldiers and supplies across open spaces in the absence of a ramp. The vehicle can readily jump to a platform of equal or lesser height. When the throttle is activated, the front of the vehicle is raised, angling the nose upward. A jet engine located in the rear center of the vehicle supplies an extra boost to reach vertical velocity when jumping to a higher plane is necessary.

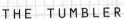

 WAYNE ENTERPRISES
APPLIED SCIENCES DIVISION
WAYNE ENTERPRISES
GAINSLY, GOTHAM, U.S.A
LUCIUS FOX

Distance from Batcave/
Wayne Manor to the center
of Gotham City is 11.9 miles;
at top speed GPD headquarters
can be reached in under 5
minutes without using the
Tumbler's jet engine.

TM & © DC Comics.   (s12)

16:14:11   04012006

GTHM GARAGE:000000

The Tumbler's shock-absorption system ensures stability. Extended front wheels help to cushion the vehicle upon impact and slow it to manageable speeds. Another key design detail is the vehicle's aerodynamic profile: airflow is directed to concentrate pressure, allowing the Tumbler to travel at significantly faster speeds than a regular vehicle of that size and shape. If needed, it can crush other vehicles under its wheels and essentially function as a tank.

Ancillary damage to public property is an unfortunate consequence of field operations, but precautions are taken to protect pedestrians; despite its bulk, the Tumbler handles incredibly well. It has bulletproof armor and is equipped with defensive and offensive weaponry, including missile launchers. The Tumbler can be activated via a handheld starter, and a driverless autopilot program utilizes preprogrammed routes throughout the city.

Lucius Fox had developed a fleet of prototype Tumblers with varying weapon configurations, ready for use, which were stored hidden at Wayne Enterprises.

TUMBLER SPECIFICATIONS

WEIGHT:	2.5 TONS
MAX. SPEED:	200+ MPH
ACCELERATION:	0 to 60 MPH IN 2.9 SECONDS
LENGTH:	15 FT
WIDTH:	9 FT, 4 IN
HEIGHT:	5 FT, 2 IN
ENGINE:	1500 HP JET TURBINE
FUEL:	GASOLINE/NITRO METHANE
JET FUEL:	LIQUID PROPANE

TM & © DC Comics.   (s12)

SECTION VEHICLES
PAGE 74

PROJECT NAME	CONTRACT NO.
TUMBLER	0640SM
INTERNAL PROJECT NO.	SERIAL NO.
JIN320256	11-1207

WAYNE ENTERPRISES APPLIED SCIENCES DIVISION

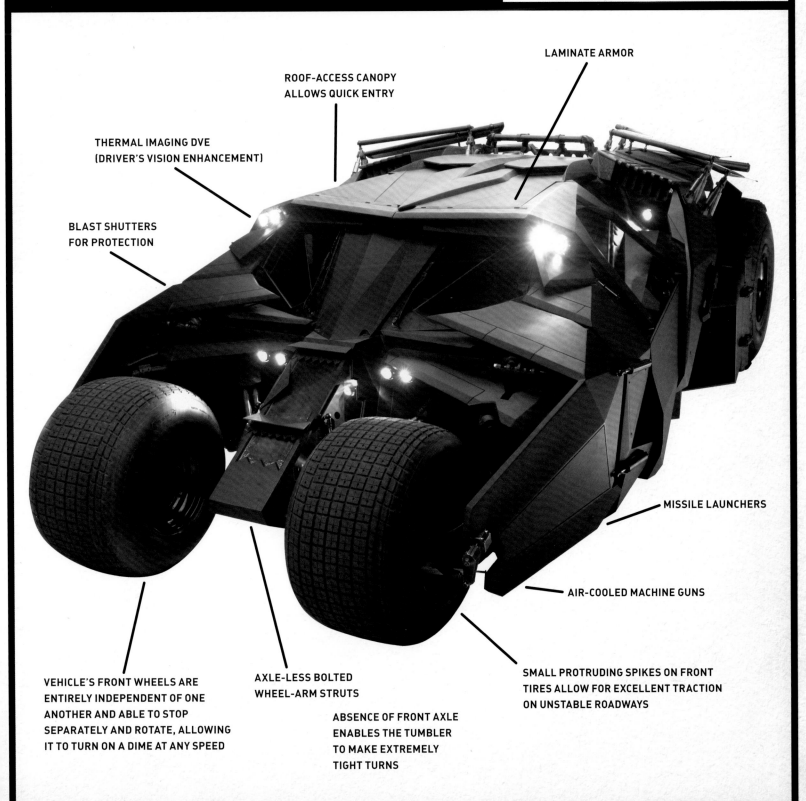

LAMINATE ARMOR

ROOF-ACCESS CANOPY
ALLOWS QUICK ENTRY

THERMAL IMAGING DVE
(DRIVER'S VISION ENHANCEMENT)

BLAST SHUTTERS
FOR PROTECTION

MISSILE LAUNCHERS

AIR-COOLED MACHINE GUNS

VEHICLE'S FRONT WHEELS ARE
ENTIRELY INDEPENDENT OF ONE
ANOTHER AND ABLE TO STOP
SEPARATELY AND ROTATE, ALLOWING
IT TO TURN ON A DIME AT ANY SPEED

AXLE-LESS BOLTED
WHEEL-ARM STRUTS

ABSENCE OF FRONT AXLE
ENABLES THE TUMBLER
TO MAKE EXTREMELY
TIGHT TURNS

SMALL PROTRUDING SPIKES ON FRONT
TIRES ALLOW FOR EXCELLENT TRACTION
ON UNSTABLE ROADWAYS

TUMBLER
CNT NO. CK1011 **PT. NO.** AW-09867

PROJECT NAME	CONTRACT NO.
TUMBLER	06405M

INTERNAL PROJECT NO.	SERIAL NO.
JIN320256	11-1207

WAYNE ENTERPRISES APPLIED SCIENCES DIVISION

FORWARD, REAR, AND SIDE HYDRAULIC AIR FOLDS
(WHICH ACT AS TINY WINGS) PUSH THE VEHICLE
DOWNWARD, CONCENTRATING AIRFLOW THROUGH THE
UNDERCARRIAGE AND ACHIEVING GREATER VELOCITY

MATTE BLACK PAINT JOB

INERTIAL REEL LANDING HOOK CAN ALSO BE
USED FOR HIGH-SPEED BREAKING

EXPLOSIVE
REACTIVE
ARMOR

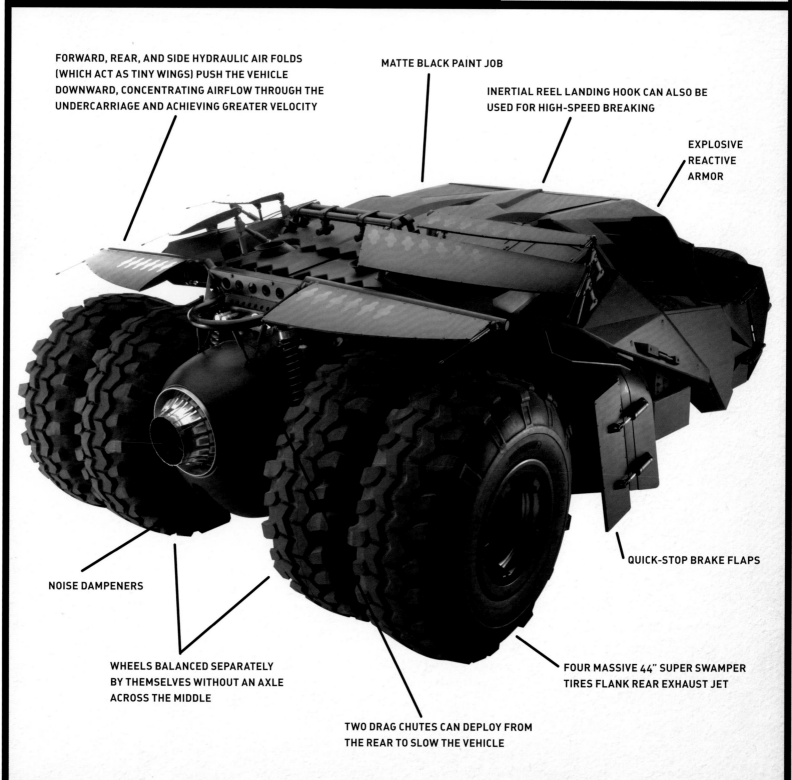

QUICK-STOP BRAKE FLAPS

NOISE DAMPENERS

WHEELS BALANCED SEPARATELY
BY THEMSELVES WITHOUT AN AXLE
ACROSS THE MIDDLE

FOUR MASSIVE 44" SUPER SWAMPER
TIRES FLANK REAR EXHAUST JET

TWO DRAG CHUTES CAN DEPLOY FROM
THE REAR TO SLOW THE VEHICLE

- HIGH-DEFINITION MONITORS GIVE MULTIANGLE VIEWS OF PURSUERS

- POLARIZED AND UNPOLARIZED BULLET-PROOF GLASS FOR PROTECTION

- AIR FILTERS FOR CHEMICAL, BIOLOGICAL, OR NUCLEAR WEAPON ATTACKS

- REARVIEW VIDEO-MONITORING SYSTEM FOR SEEING ATTACKS FROM BEHIND

- RADIO IN VEHICLE TO MONITOR POLICE BANDS, COMMUNICATE WITH ALFRED

- ONBOARD VOICE ACTIVATION

- ADDITIONAL PASSENGER SEATING

- HOLOGRAM GENERATOR FOR 3-D IMAGING AND ONE-TOUCH CONTROLS

- VOICE-RECOGNITION MICRO-PHONE AND INTERNAL SPEAKERS

- SATELLITE NAVIGATION UPLINK AND GPS GLOBAL-POSITIONING SYSTEM INCLUDES THOROUGH MAPS OF GOTHAM'S ALLEYS, STREETS, SUBTERRAIN, AND ROOFTOPS

TUMBLER COCKPIT
CNT NO. RG-10117 **PT. NO.** IE-10867

PROJECT NAME	CONTRACT NO.
TUMBLER COCKPIT	06405M
INTERNAL PROJECT NO.	SERIAL NO.
WRE68FRFX	06-0598

WAYNE ENTERPRISES APPLIED SCIENCES DIVISION

- CONTROLS INCLUDE: INERTIA REEL DEPLOY, JET VECTOR MANEUVERING, AFTERBURNER TOGGLE, AN ARRAY OF COMMS, SLIDING-ARMOR FORWARD SIGHTS

- MULTICONTROL JOYSTICK IS SENSITIVE TO SLIGHT MOVEMENTS, LOCATED IN STEERING COLUMN OF MOTORIZED SEAT GURNEY AND GIVES DRIVER EASE IN HIGH-SPEED PURSUITS

- COCKPIT CAN SHIFT AND UNFOLD INTO A FORWARD DRIVING POSITION FOR SPECIAL MANEUVERS SUCH AS USING THE GUIDED MISSILES

- AIR BAGS FOR POSSIBLE IMPACT

- COCKPIT SEAT IS MOTORIZED, SEGMENTED, AND MADE OF SUPER-STRONG COMPOSITE METAL ALLOY

- COCKPIT POD IS GYROSCOPICALLY BALANCED, KEEPING THE DRIVER VERTICALLY INCLINED REGARDLESS OF THE VEHICLE'S ANGLE

TUMBLER
CNT NO. CKI0II PT. NO. AW-09867

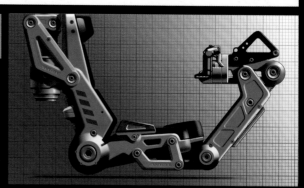

PROJECT NAME	CONTRACT NO.
TUMBLER COCKPIT	94930

INTERNAL PROJECT NO.	SERIAL NO.
KKY-110506	06-0598

WAYNE ENTERPRISES APPLIED SCIENCES DIVISION

STEALTH MODE

During "Silent Running" or "Stealth" mode, employed when a discreet getaway or arrival is needed, the engine switches to electric to reduce noise. Halogen spotlights are turned off, and the angled exterior of the Tumbler makes radar tracking difficult. Nighttime navigation is enhanced using technology derived from night-vision goggles, and the "Loiter" setting utilizes a "ghost driver" to give the appearance of activity. The "Intimidate" setting used for threatening an enemy is capable of firing missiles to destroy barricades or structural obstacles.

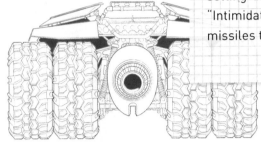

JET POWER

In addition to its regular engine, the Tumbler has a second propane-fueled jet engine, which provides over 3,000 lbs of thrust to the vehicle's high-powered jumps. An armored hull protects the explosive fuel tanks, which can be quickly cut off via switches located in the cockpit. These tanks can also be expelled safely during travel should they rupture or become a liability.

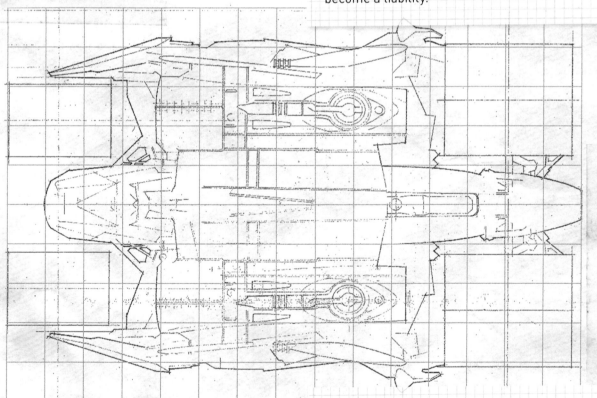

WEAPONS

The console display is used to control the cannons in the nose of the vehicle, which fire standard ballistic missiles as well as a variety of nonlethal rounds, tear-gas shells, fire-retardant gel canisters, and sticky foam. A strip of tensile plastic studded with metal spikes can drop from rear of vehicle to deter enemy chase.

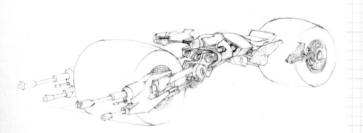

TUMBLER ESCAPE POD

In the event that the Tumbler suffered catastrophic damage, field contingencies had to be in place. A mechanism to initiate an eject sequence from within the cockpit was developed, allowing a two-wheeled motorbike to eject from the damaged vehicle and function on its own. This "Pod" is sleek, raw, and formidable in its own right. When piloting the vehicle, one must lean forward to guide it, a technique used by professional racers to lessen drag, thereby increasing speed. Additionally, a lower center of gravity gives the driver greater control over the Pod, allowing him to steer by shifting body weight as needed for maneuvers. This posture also lessens exposure to gunfire.

TUMBLER ESCAPE POD
CNT NO. RGIIII **PT. NO.** IE-027563

PROJECT NAME	CONTRACT NO.
POD	06405M
INTERNAL PROJECT NO.	SERIAL NO.
SNP326416	II-1327

WAYNE ENTERPRISES APPLIED SCIENCES DIVISION

NO SEATING AREA; LEGS SPLAYED APART BY 3 FEET

ARM SHIELDS ON HANDLE-BARS OFFER PROTECTION

NO EXTERNAL EXHAUST; ENGINE/CHASSIS IS EXHAUST SYSTEM

WEIGHS OVER 700 LBS

EMP RIFLE MOUNT

A STANDARD BIKE HAS SINGLE ENGINE IN CENTER BUT THE POD HAS TWO ENGINES, ONE IN HUB ON FRONT WHEEL AND THE OTHER LOCATED IN BACK WHEEL

RADIATOR DOUBLES AS FOOT PADS

PREPROGRAMMED COMPUTER CONTROLS TWO-ENGINE/WHEEL SYSTEM FOR PRECISE SYNCHRONIZATION

AUTO-AIRCRAFT GUN LOCATED PROXIMALLY ON WHEELS

HYDRAULIC ARM ENABLES BROAD RANGE OF MOTION

WHEEL POSITION AND GUN MOUNT AUTO-SYNC

TUMBLER ESCAPE POD / SIMULATION
CNT NO. HH3247 PT. NO. HY-111108

PROJECT NAME	CONTRACT NO.
POD / SIMULATION	1224TYR

INTERNAL PROJECT NO.	SERIAL NO.
WST101446	11-1327

WAYNE ENTERPRISES APPLIED SCIENCES DIVISION

THE POD RELIES ON A STATE-OF-THE-ART DRIVE TRAIN FOR EXPLOSIVE SPEED AND ACCELERATION. IT UTILIZES THE TUMBLER'S FRONT WHEELS, WHICH REMAIN INDEPENDENT OF ONE ANOTHER. THIS ALLOWS THE RIDER TO PIVOT SHARPLY WHILE MAINTAINING SPEED AND CONTROL ON MOST TERRAIN.

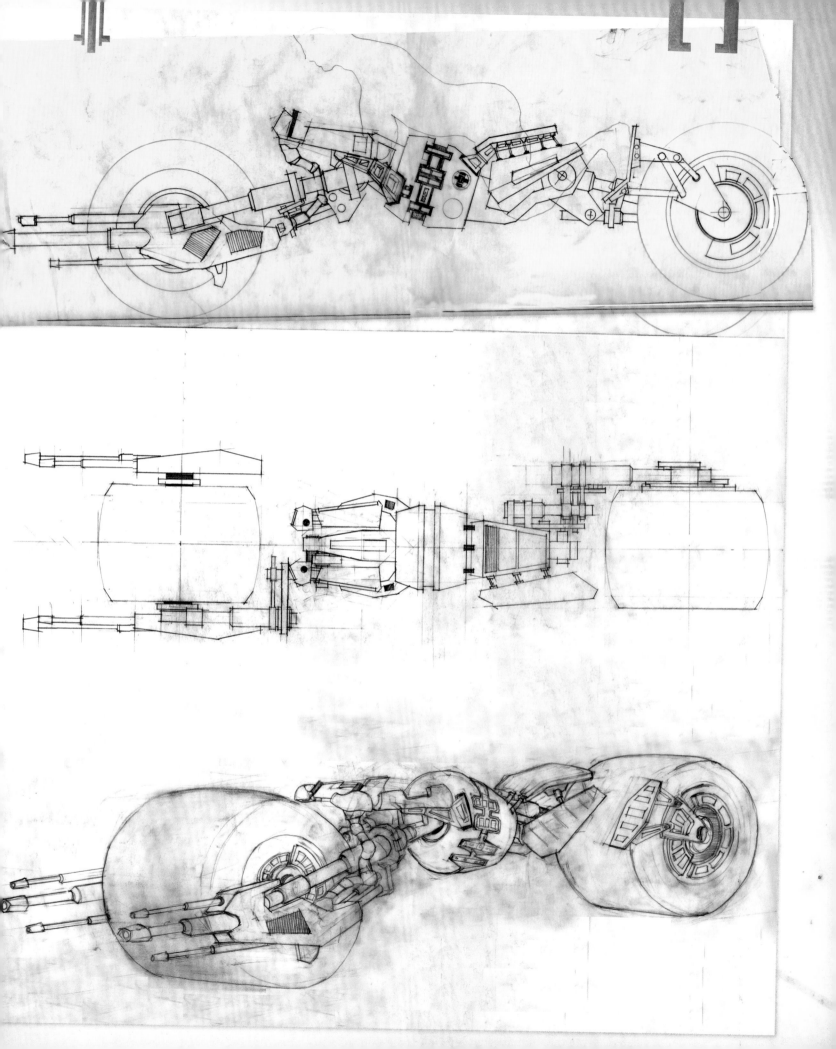

THE BAT

Lucius Fox encouraged the use of a prototype air vehicle that Wayne Enterprises once developed for the Department of Defense. It was created as a tool for urban pacification and could handle tight geometric maneuvers between buildings without recirculation. Fox dubbed it "the Bat." The craft has large propellers on either side of its undercarriage, which create a vortex of air and lift the vehicle off the ground. The dual rotor downdraft from the propellers can also function as a weapon. The cyclonic winds from the spinning blades have the power to force individuals to the ground and cause general disruption to an area.

The Bat's autopilot function, which effectively kills the floodlights and shuts down the craft's main engines, allowing it to quietly hover through sensitive areas, is currently disabled.

TWO-PERSON COCKPIT DESIGN
GIVES PILOTS MAXIMUM CONTROL

DUAL-MOUNTED FLOODLIGHTS

SIDE PANEL ROCKET LAUNCHERS
BREAK THROUGH ROCK OR METAL

DUAL-ANCHORED
MACHINE GUNS FUNCTION
AS A DETERRENT

EMP CANNON GUIDANCE MOUNT
FIRES BURSTS TO DISRUPT
ELECTRONIC TRANSMISSIONS

THE BAT: FRONT VIEW
CNT NO. CK1011 **PT. NO.** AW-09867

PROJECT NAME	CONTRACT NO.
THE BAT: FRONT VIEW	04890
INTERNAL PROJECT NO.	SERIAL NO.
10PDR	11-1208

WAYNE ENTERPRISES APPLIED SCIENCES DIVISION

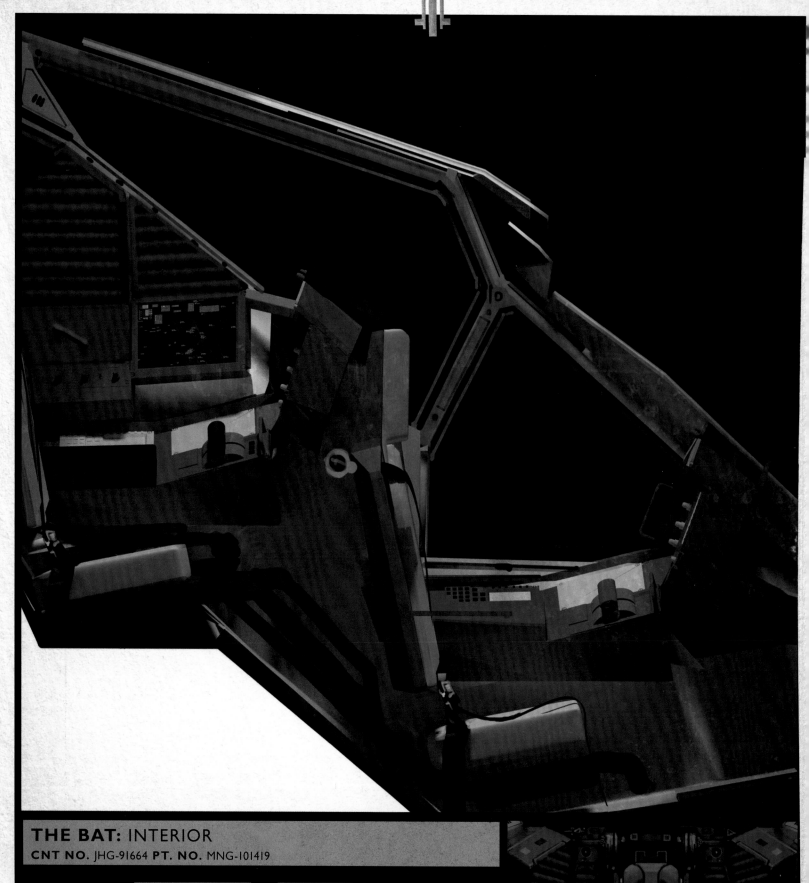

THE BAT: INTERIOR
CNT NO. JHG-91664 **PT. NO.** MNG-101419

PROJECT NAME	CONTRACT NO.
THE BAT: INTERIOR	04890

INTERNAL PROJECT NO.	SERIAL NO.
10PDR	11-1208

WAYNE ENTERPRISES APPLIED SCIENCES DIVISION

POLICE
VEHICLE IDENTIFICATION
TDK2012

THIS VEHICLE IS ON OFFICIAL
GOTHAM CITY BUSINESS

SWAT

GOTHAM CITY

FIRE DEPT.
VEHICLE IDENTIFICATION
TDK2012

THIS VEHICLE IS ON OFFICIAL
GOTHAM CITY BUSINESS

BAT SYMBOL

CITY OF GOTHAM
POLICE DEPARTMENT
38th PCT

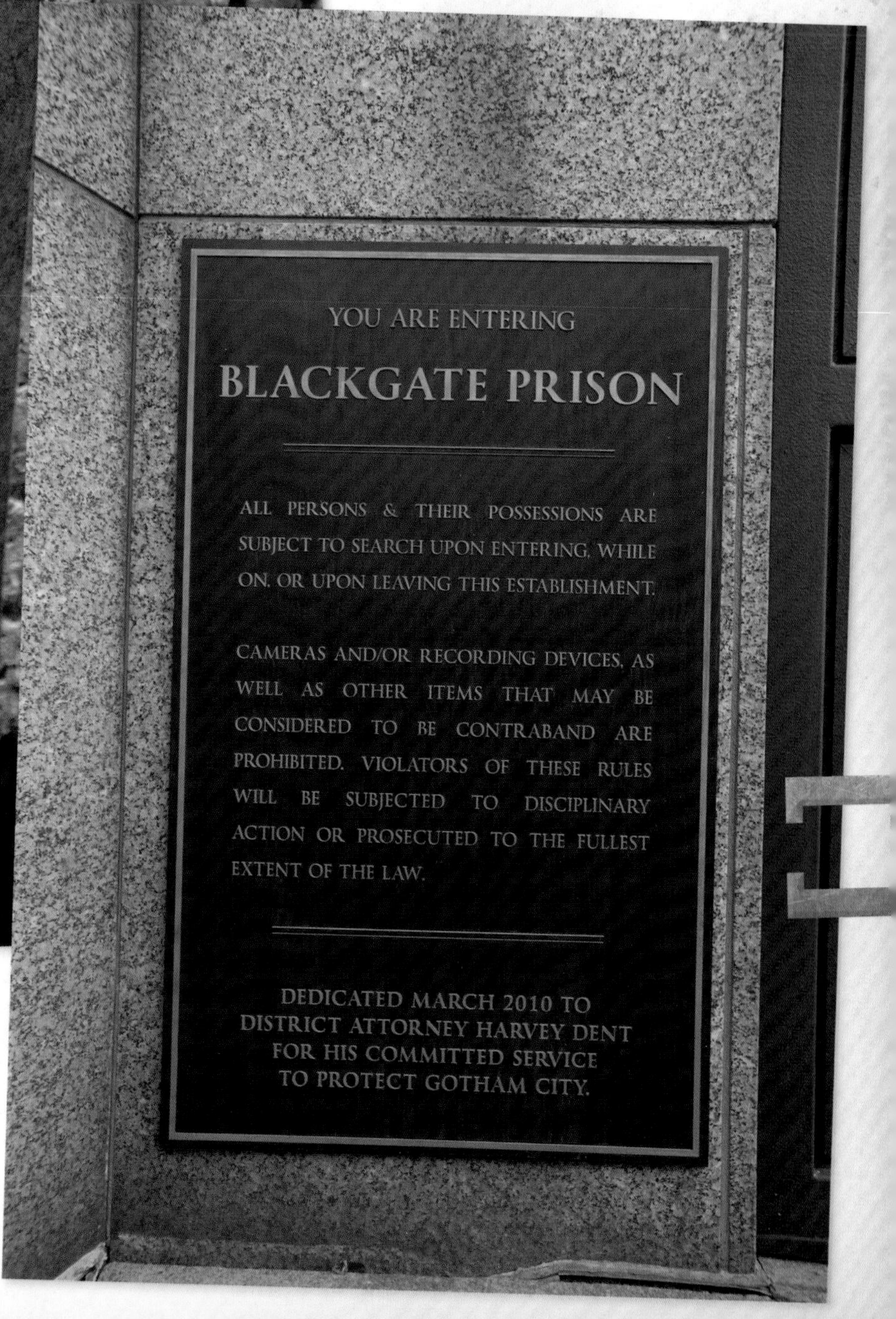

YOU ARE ENTERING

BLACKGATE PRISON

ALL PERSONS & THEIR POSSESSIONS ARE
SUBJECT TO SEARCH UPON ENTERING, WHILE
ON, OR UPON LEAVING THIS ESTABLISHMENT.

CAMERAS AND/OR RECORDING DEVICES, AS
WELL AS OTHER ITEMS THAT MAY BE
CONSIDERED TO BE CONTRABAND ARE
PROHIBITED. VIOLATORS OF THESE RULES
WILL BE SUBJECTED TO DISCIPLINARY
ACTION OR PROSECUTED TO THE FULLEST
EXTENT OF THE LAW.

DEDICATED MARCH 2010 TO
DISTRICT ATTORNEY HARVEY DENT
FOR HIS COMMITTED SERVICE
TO PROTECT GOTHAM CITY.

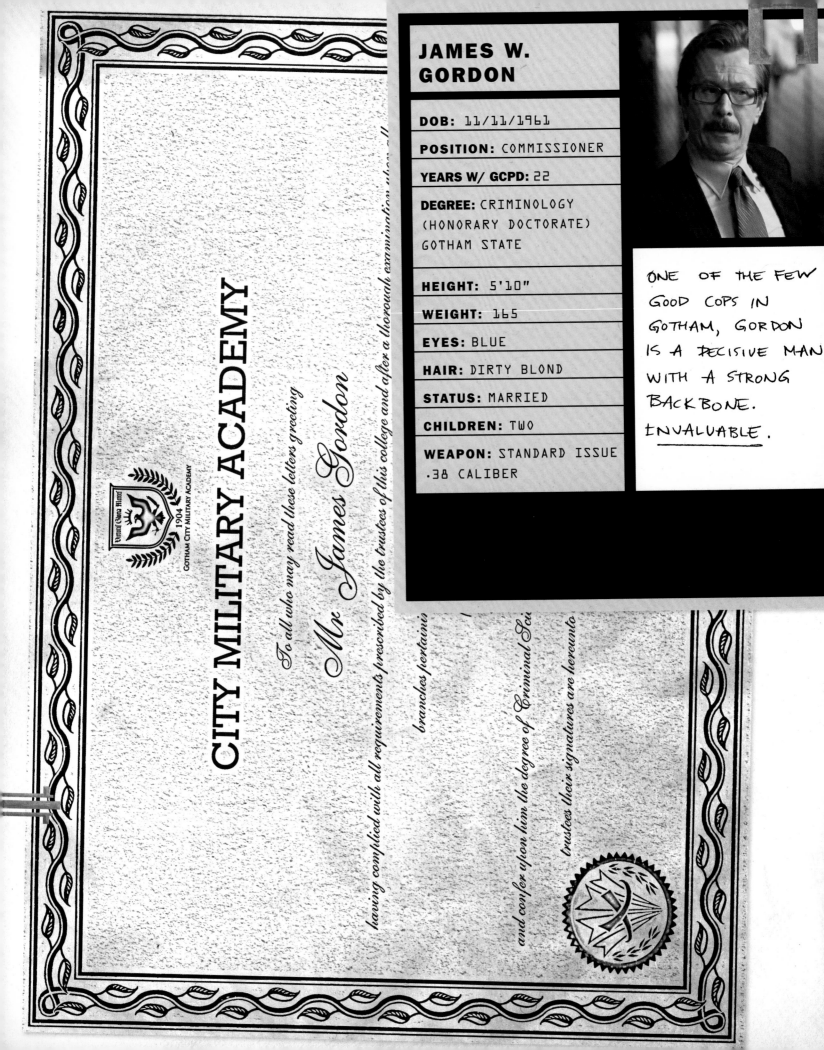

CITY MILITARY ACADEMY

To all who may read these letters greeting

Mr. James Gordon

having complied with all requirements prescribed by the trustees of this college and after a thorough examination upon all

branches pertaining

and confer upon him the degree of Criminal Science

trustees their signatures are hereunto

GOTHAM CITY MILITARY ACADEMY

1904

JAMES W. GORDON

DOB: 11/11/1961

POSITION: COMMISSIONER

YEARS W/ GCPD: 22

DEGREE: CRIMINOLOGY (HONORARY DOCTORATE) GOTHAM STATE

HEIGHT: 5'10"

WEIGHT: 165

EYES: BLUE

HAIR: DIRTY BLOND

STATUS: MARRIED

CHILDREN: TWO

WEAPON: STANDARD ISSUE .38 CALIBER

ONE OF THE FEW GOOD COPS IN GOTHAM, GORDON IS A DECISIVE MAN WITH A STRONG BACKBONE. INVALUABLE.

TUMB. CAM2

01122008

POLICE
VEHICLES
ONLY

THE GPD/JAMES GORDON

Thorough investigations into the Gotham Police Department originally yielded disappointing results. Hours were spent cataloging, observing, and surveying their members, and the conclusion was that many were not to be trusted. Officers around the department had their dirty hands in mob dealings across the city. It might have been easy to find one that could be finessed into feeding me information, but the best route was finding someone who had strong moral footing and then appealing to his sense of justice.

It was a difficult search, but Jim Gordon proved to be this man. His quick thinking and judgment stood out among his colleagues, and it eventually catapulted him into a leadership position as Commissioner. His honor and courage in the line of duty gained the trust of the department and the faith of Gotham City's leadership.

DISTRICT ATTORN
OF THE
CITY OF GOTHAM

HARVEY DENT
DISTRICT ATTORNEY

MEMORANDUM OF AGREEMENT BETW
DEPARTMENT OF CORRECTIONAL SERVIC
ATTORNEY'S OFFICE

This agreement is hereby entered into between the Goth
Correctional Services (also referred to as GDCS) and the
referred to as the DA) regarding a cooperative working a
of inmate maltreatment.

GDCS is charged under NCGS 0A-180 to establish prote

HARVEY DENT

DOB: 08/09/1965

DOD: 06/15/2004

AFFILIATION: INDEPENDENT

HEIGHT: 6'1"

WEIGHT: 175

EYES: BLUE

HAIR: BLOND

STATUS: SINGLE

CHILDREN: NONE

HARVEY DENT

Gotham City officials are a hard group of people to trust. Many of them believe in the basic principles of justice but have grown exhausted fighting an uphill battle. In a town where criminal money can sway even the purest of souls, there aren't many figures for the people to look up to. When Harvey Dent took office as Gotham's new District Attorney, he set out to dismantle the stranglehold that organized crime had on the city. He acted quickly and decisively with passion and force. He was fair-minded and driven—a figurehead of criminal justice. As Batman, I sought an alliance with Dent, an advocate in the public sector that I could trust.

SECTION: PROFILES
PAGE: 92

CARMINE FALCONE

DOB: 07/01/1947

AFFILIATION: MAFIA

HEIGHT: 6'

WEIGHT: 185 LBS

EYES: HAZEL

HAIR: LIGHT BROWN

CARMINE FALCONE

Carmine Falcone was Gotham's premier crime boss for decades, and under his influence the city decayed to the point where its citizens began to lose any hope for its recovery. His reach extended to the highest levels of Gotham's police department, its courts, and its businesses. Few were spared Falcone's corruptive grasp, and those who did knew they were hopelessly outnumbered. His tyrannical rule was responsible for unraveling all the improvements to Gotham made by Thomas Wayne and his Wayne Foundation. In the years after Thomas and Martha Wayne's murder at the hands of Joe Chill, a man forced to turn to a life of crime to survive in Falcone's world, Gotham became a symbol of stagnation and apathy.

It was only when Batman made his first appearance that the tide finally turned. Falcone was arrested with irrefutable evidence, and it looked like order could finally be restored to a population that desperately needed it. But before much could come of Falcone's incarceration, he was deemed clinically insane and sent to Arkham Asylum under the questionable care of Dr. Jonathan Crane, later the villain known as the Scarecrow. Salvatore Maroni then assumed control of what was left of the Falcone crime family.

JOHN BLAKE

POSITION: SERGEANT

YEARS W/ GPD: 1

DEGREE:
A.A. CRIMINAL JUSTICE

HEIGHT: 5'10"

WEIGHT: 160 LBS

EYES: BROWN

HAIR: BROWN

STATUS: SINGLE

CHILDREN: NONE

WEAPON:
STD. ISSUE .38 CALIBER

JOHN BLAKE

My role as Gotham's self-appointed protector can be isolating. I rarely extend myself to those outside my small circle of allies but in recent times I've been forced to reassess my old ways in order to fully combat threats against the city. A young officer on the Gotham police force named John Blake has shown me that, despite the hurdles I confront, my mission is true and right. Blake himself is an orphan and has faced his share of hardships. Unlike me, he didn't have the wealth and opportunity to facilitate a concentrated crime-fighting operation but that didn't stop him from committing himself to the ideal of justice. He's channeled his anger and pain, as I did, into his work serving and protecting the people of Gotham. Under the guidance of Jim Gordon, Blake has flourished. His passion and precision haven't gone unnoticed and he has become an asset to the city.

MIRANDA TATE

DOB: 9/30/1978

DEGREE: MBA, KELLOGG

HEIGHT: 5'7"

WEIGHT: 120 LBS

EYES: BROWN

HAIR: BROWN

CHILDREN: NONE

MIRANDA TATE

In order to concentrate on my mission, I've entrusted a select team of forward-thinking individuals to guide Wayne Enterprises and its endeavors while I focus on my other pursuits. Among those individuals is Miranda Tate, an incredibly intelligent, savvy businesswoman to whom I immediately found myself drawn. Miranda has been instrumental in guiding the company on a progressive, environmentally friendly path. And, as a shareholder in Wayne Enterprises, Miranda has an important seat on the Board of Directors. She and I share a vision for Gotham that includes limitless energy without the harmful effects to humanity. Miranda brings with her a global way of thinking and one day soon, perhaps together, we'll be able to bring our vision to fruition.

Gotham City is home to a number of mentally unstable and sociopathic criminals. These troubling individuals have often used theatrical devices as well as chemical warfare in their quest for underworld dominance; their arsenals are often tied to their damaged mental state in both form and function. Some enemies favor harsh methods of torture, while others seek to dismantle the mind.

ARKM 1111 INT. RM

09:16   060598KYG

JONATHAN CRANE

DOB: 10/20/1973

EMPLOYMENT HISTORY:
GOTHAM UNIVERSITY;
ARKHAM ASYLUM

HEIGHT: 5'10"

WEIGHT: 165

EYES: BLUE

HAIR: LIGHT BROWN

STATUS: SINGLE

CHILDREN: NONE

JONATHAN CRANE AKA THE SCARECROW

Once a Gotham University professor, and an expert of psychopharmacology, Dr. Jonathan Crane was deposed from the institution due to his highly controversial experimentation on his subjects. Despite having lost the respect of his colleagues, Crane's work on the chemical effects of unadulterated fear on the human mind and body gained the attention of administrators at Arkham Asylum, who promoted him to chief administrator of the facility.

Crane built a strong reputation and his professional opinion became valued by the city's legal structure, which made him quite attractive to mob leader Carmine Falcone. Crane's rumored experimentation with psychotropic drugs also made him vulnerable to blackmail. Falcone drafted Crane and gave him a specific purpose within the crime organization: When his men passed through the court system, Crane would have them deemed insane in order to keep them out of prison. In exchange, Falcone would help Crane move shipments of his psychotropic drugs into the city.

Crane's interest in the subject of fear spiraled into obsession. He adopted the persona of the Scarecrow, a mask he wore when committing crimes and when dealing with Falcone's men.

Rā's ⟷ CRANE

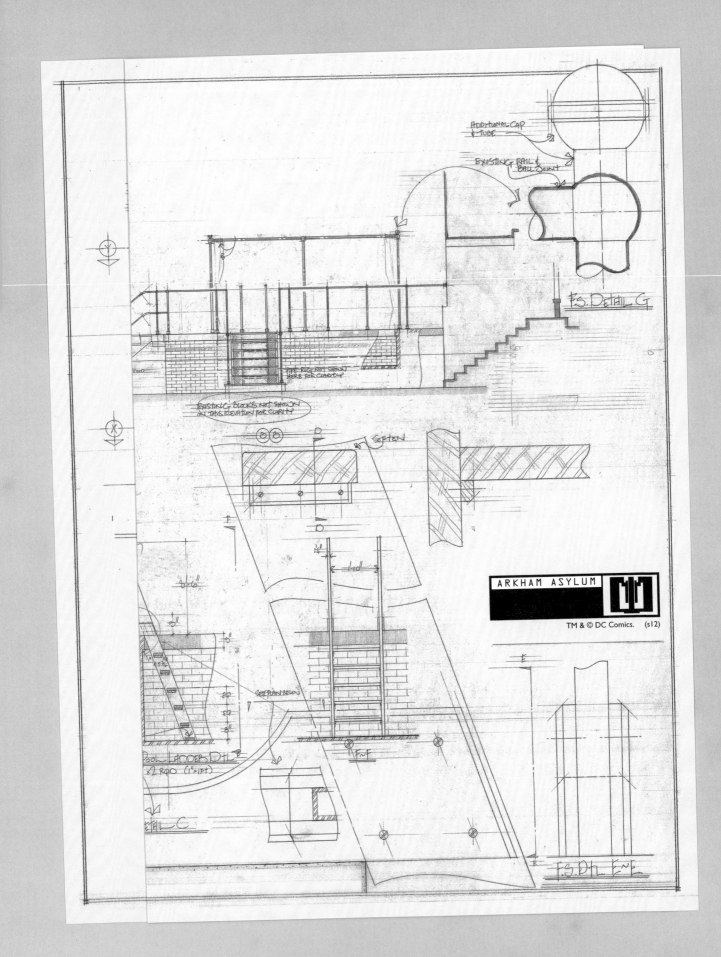

ADDITIONAL CAP
& TUBE

EXISTING RAIL &
BALL JOINT

F.S. DETAIL G

PIPE RIG NOT SHOWN
HERE FOR CLARITY

EXISTING BLOCKS NOT SHOWN
ON THIS ELEVATION FOR CLARITY

SOFTEN

SEE PLAN BELOW

POOL LADDER DTL
X 2 RQD (1"=1FT)

DETAIL G

ARKHAM ASYLUM

TM & © DC Comics.   (s12)

F.S. DTL E'N'E

ARKHAM ASYLUM

ANALYST: **Dr. Jonathan Crane**

FINAL EVALUATION: **Victor Zsasz**

After continued evaluation of Victor Zsasz and the criminal charges leveled against him by the District Attorney's office of Gotham City, I have come to the conclusion that Mr. Zsasz is of unfit mind and should be remanded to Arkham Asylum for further psychiatric evaluation. Despite the severity of Mr. Zsasz's crimes, I believe that the source of his violence is clearly the result of a fractured mind brought about by a damaging childhood.

The loss of Mr. Zsasz's parents at a young age had a profound effect on the only child. His father, once a prominent businessman in Gotham City, squandered his money through a severe gambling addiction. When both his mother and father died, Victor was left with no money and no family and was therefore placed in the foster system, where violence, bullying, and terror were standard conditions. In this environment, he developed an irreparably skewed sense of morality.

In Victor's case, that legacy made him an easy recruit for the Falcone syndicate. My professional opinion holds that Victor did not seek out this life of crime because he enjoyed inflicting violence. Rather, he turned to organized crime because it was the only family he had ever truly known. Having lost his father at a young age, and without the support of his parents to guide him, Victor sought the approval of the only father figure in his life: Carmine Falcone. The only way to earn that father figure's trust and affection was to hurt people. Every action taken by Victor Zsasz that brought him before the ire of the court was taken in an attempt to earn the adoration he was denied in childhood.

Given these findings, I believe the only humane way to proceed is to submit Mr. Zsasz to my asylum for intensive psychiatric care. Only then may we be able to effectively treat the disease that eats at his mind.

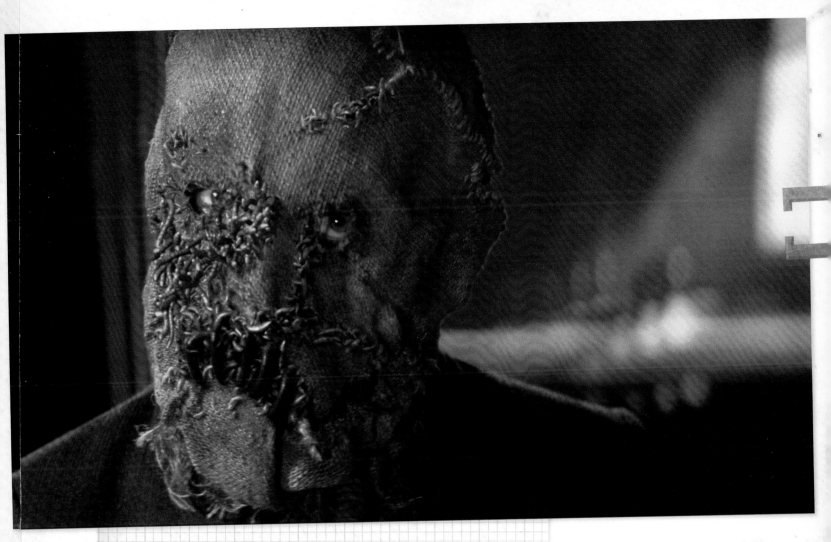

THE SCARECROW'S FEAR TOXIN & MASK

As the Scarecrow, Crane created a dangerous hallucinogenic substance capable of latching onto his subjects' greatest fears and overwhelming them with psychotic images. This "fear toxin" was derived from the blue flower growing near Rā's al Ghūl's Bhutan monastery. The substance was inconspicuous enough to be smuggled into the US inside a shipment of stuffed animals yet potent enough to cause widespread destruction. Crane partnered with Rā's al Ghūl to develop a personal delivery system that transformed this toxin into an ejectable gas, which could be emitted from a tube in his sleeve or from his mask. What appeared to be a simple burlap sack with eyehole slits and a noose-style closure at the neck hid a decompressible device that allows for a timed release of fear toxin. The mask also served to protect Crane from the effects of the substance.

   Among the victims of Crane's fear toxin were Falcone's men and, ultimately, Falcone himself.

THE JOKER

The Joker's actions belied a diabolical, anarchic mentality and a complete absence of human empathy. He arrived as an unknown quantity, using methods that confounded even the established criminal underworld. In this sense, the Joker offered the criminals of Gotham something untested but strangely rational. They saw in him a shared vision of Batman's destruction. Despite his clearly unstable mental state, this was enough to foster a deadly alliance.

The cause of the Joker's ferocious scarring remains unknown, but he used his disfigurement to his advantage—to distract and throw others off balance. Disturbing clownlike makeup helped to mask his identity and heighten the mystery and unpredictability about him. Like his appearance, his actions were riddled with contradictions and a perverted sense of whimsy. The playing cards he left around the city are a prime example.

EVIDENCE

CITY OF GOTHAM POLICE DEPARTMENT

CITY OF GOTHAM POLICE DEPARTMENT

EVIDENCE

THE JOKER'S CARDS

CASE FILE

H. Green	Records		5/1/06	
~~P.H. Grosstberg~~	~~Released to Office~~		~~1/10/07 2:11 pm~~	
GCC Recieving	George Hollis CMD		2 24 07	9:23 am
George Hollis, CMD	Coroner's Office		2/25/07	10:47 am
Timmons/Records Dept.	Document Reproduction		3-12-08	6:38 pm
Stavros Merrimani: DR	Records: Keeting,		3/13/08	11 02
Gherry Csupor LAB 234	G. Biryani: Lab Review		3/19/08	9:54 am
S.G.A's Office: L. Kitt	Farah Minerj S.A.O	April 4th 2008		9:54am
Sonia F. / Records	Doc. Repro		7-14-08	6:38 pm

GOTHAM POLICE DEPARTMENT

JOKER'S CRIMES, KNOWN AND SUSPECTED, LEADING UP TO HIS INCARCERATION:

Armed robbery with double homicide (first recorded appearance of the Joker playing card).

Coordinated bank heist, multiple homicides, including the men he employed to carry out the crime.

Murder of six uniformed officers of the GPD.

Murder of Gotham City resident Brian Douglas, survived by wife (Deborah) and son (Anthony).

B&E, kidnapping, and assault at the site of Bruce Wayne fundraiser for Harvey Dent. Attempted murder of Assistant DA Rachel Dawes.

Suspected in the murders of Judge Surrillo and Police Commissioner Loeb and attempted murder of District Attorney Harvey Dent.

Suspected in the murder of Southside crime boss known in Gotham's criminal circles as "Gambol."

Suspected in the murders of Gotham residents Richard Dent and Patrick Harvey. The victims have no apparent connection to the Joker other than their last names combining to read "Harvey Dent."

Attempted murder of Lieutenant James Gordon and conspiracy to assassinate the mayor.

Murder of Assistant DA Rachel Dawes.

Second attempted murder of DA Harvey Dent.

IDENTITY

The Joker has been taken into custody but we are still no closer to ascertaining his identity.

Many of the men we've taken into custody in association with his crimes are former patients at Arkham Asylum. We suspect that the Joker himself is a former patient, yet the Asylum has no record of him.

The Joker does not appear to have any connection to Gotham's crime syndicates, though he knocked over a mob bank. One possible motive for this, which could also explain the clown motif, is the Haley Brothers Circus. The circus was recently in town for a two-month engagement and it was rumored their boss had connections to Sal Maroni. The Joker could be a former Haley Brothers employee with some kind of grudge against the mob.

Given the Joker's access to, and relative comfort with, military-grade technology such as grapple cannons, weaponized gases, explosives, and automatic weapons, it is possible that the man is a former soldier, perhaps suffering from severe PTSD.

POSSIBLE MOTIVES

Consolidation of power—The Joker could be trying to eliminate any mob control over Gotham so he can install himself as the supreme crime boss in town.

Anarchy—The Joker has murdered or attempted to murder various civic officials. It's possible that he is an extremist anti-government agitator or a soldier angry with the government for sending him to war.

Mayhem—The Joker's actions suggest he may simply incite violence for violence's sake.

CLASSIFIED

The Joker's go-to tactic involved putting his enemies' loved ones in peril. I must assume he did this in order to observe and size up his adversaries based on how they responded.

But the response of Gotham's citizenship was not what the Joker anticipated, and witnessing his own folly cut any tether he may have had to reality. His descent into madness led to his capture—but not before he had established himself as one of the most formidable sociopaths Gotham has ever known.

PROFILES

1◊1

BANE

DOB: UNKNOWN

HEIGHT: 6'1"

WEIGHT: 240 LBS

EYES: BLUE

HAIR: UNKNOWN

ORIGINS: UNKNOWN

FIGHTING STYLE:
RESULT-BASED; BRUTAL;
EXTREMELY DANGEROUS

INTELLIGENCE LEVEL:
EXTREMELY HIGH

BANE

Details surrounding Bane's origins are vague at best. What is known is that he is an international mercenary and self-styled liberator. He's also a ferocious fighter, trained in the severest and deadliest combat disciplines known to man. Bane's physique is formidable, the result of years of strength and fight training. He can anticipate and counter an enemy's move with pinpoint precision. Bane is also a skilled tactician and has amassed a considerable army of derelicts underneath the streets of Gotham to do his dirty work. He targets the disenfranchised—men and women without homes, children without hope. He's rumored to have transformed the tunnels under the city into his private lair, filling it with his mercenary brethren who keep him protected and unswervingly do his bidding.

To date, Bane has not been reported to be seen without his mask on. The mask appears to serve as a breathing apparatus, worn to manage pain. A series of tubes supplies an uninterrupted flow of an inhalant, thought to be an opiate analgesic or similar medication. The nature of his injury is unknown.

MEDIA REPORTS NAME BANE AS THE INSTIGATOR BEHIND
A NUMBER OF ACTS OF VIOLENCE AROUND GOTHAM.
SURVEILLANCE FOOTAGE SUPPORTS BUT DOES NOT CONFIRM
ALLEGATIONS TO DATE.

HIGH ALERT

Sheet

72

20

CDL0983628   State IL

WAYNE ENTERPRISES
APPLIED SCIENCES DIVISION

CAREFUL, MASTER
WAYNE ... MS. KYLE'S TALENT
FOR MANIPULATION IS
NOT TO BE UNDERESTIMATED.
— ALFRED

SELINA KYLE

Some criminals work from the depths of the underworld and some from the top of the corporate ladder. Selina Kyle is able to seamlessly blend into either of these worlds with ease and sophistication. Her detective skills are unmatched. Selina is a mixture of contradictions: cunning and intelligent, she often resorts to simple acts of theft. Despite these traits, she sees potential in others and wishes to give back, an interesting element to note in a thief.

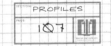

SECTION PROFILES PAGE 107

CLEAN SLATE: WE HAVE INTERCEPTED REPORTS OF A COMPUTER PROGRAM, CODE NAMED "CLEAN SLATE," THAT MAY HAVE THE ABILITY TO WIPE CLEAN A PERSON'S HISTORY FROM ANY AND ALL ELECTRONIC DEVICES AND ONLINE OCCURRENCES. BY USING THE PROGRAM, A CRIMINAL'S RECORDS COULD BE EXPUNGED AND ALL TRACES OF IMPROPRIETY DELETED. SELINA HAS EXPRESSED INTEREST IN THE CONCEPT, BUT DETAILS REMAIN UNSUBSTANTIATED.

SELINA'S ARSENAL

Selina has demonstrated a small but sophisticated arsenal of weaponry. Her belt contains basic picks and skeleton keys, used to gain entry into locked rooms and secured areas. For safecracking, she carries a listening device that fits snugly into her ear, allowing her to determine the combination of a rotary locking safe.

Selina's belt also houses a kit containing adhesives and a graphite powder, which she uses to remove fingerprints.

SELINA'S COSTUME

Selina is a chameleon and can step into a variety of roles both in her private and criminal life. Her face is sometimes covered with a basic domino mask with an attached set of goggles that rest atop her head when not in use. The goggles are outfitted with lenses that have infrared capabilities, and contain an LED source that creates low-intensity light to illuminate a variety of spectrums. This allows her to see in the dark. The formfitting black suit is a single piece made of ribbed PVC. The suit allows for a great range of motion but, lacking any armor, it's not very conducive to battle. Selina has, however, found ways to protect herself. Her boots are steel toed with a serrated stiletto heel. The heel is a perfect weapon for breaking through glass or high-kicking an opponent. She has exhibited strong hand-to-hand combat training and great acrobatic skill, but her exact training in these areas has yet to be confirmed.

WAYNE ENTERPRISES
APPLIED SCIENCES DIVISION

WAYNE ENTERPRISES
GAINSLY, GOTHAM, U.S.A.

To: Miranda Tate
From: Lucius Fox
Date: 8/9/11
Subject: WAYNE ENTERPRISES FUSION REACTOR

As natural resources dwindle, the need for innovative thinking is more important than ever. Wayne Enterprises encourages the development of high-concept environmental solutions. One such project is a clean fuel source—a new kind of safe energy poised to change the world: a fusion reactor that produces zero radiation and uses no fossil fuels. Rigorous testing is underway to eliminate all potential complications prior to launching the reactor on a global scale. Many aspects of this project are classified due to their sensitive nature.

The reactor is kept below a Wayne Enterprises recycling plant located on the Gotham River. In the event of a security breach or, in a worst-case scenario, a meltdown, the reactor can be flooded and cooled down before it reaches a critical point. Tubing and shaft-ways lead directly to the device and can funnel river water into the reactor's core were its temperature to reach critical levels. Entry into the reactor is marked by a tamper-proof fingerprint identifier to prevent infiltration.

Keeping a project of this magnitude in operation has cost Wayne Enterprises considerable funding, but, if successful, the ultimate yield will be immeasurable.

FUSION REACTOR

CNT NO. KK-III165 **PT. NO.** 25027W

PERPENDICULAR RINGS OF ELECTROMAGNETS SUSPENDED
BY A BOWLING BALL—SIZED MASS OF METAL

PROJECT NAME	CONTRACT NO.
FUSION REACTOR	BRD201112

INTERNAL PROJECT NO.	SERIAL NO.
CC1313	**KDS-II-65**

WAYNE ENTERPRISES APPLIED SCIENCES DIVISION